HOME BUYERS

Lambs to the Slaughter?

HOME BUYERS
Lambs to the Slaughter?

Sloan Bashinsky

Menasha Ridge Press
Hillsborough, North Carolina
Distributed by Simon & Schuster

Published by Menasha Ridge Press
Hillsborough, North Carolina

Library of Congress Cataloging in Publication Data

Bashinsky, Sloan, 1942–
  Home buyers.

  Includes index.
  1. House buying.   2. Real estate business.   I. Title.
HD1379.B37   643'.12   84-6692
ISBN 0-89732-027-1
ISBN 0-671-55729-7 Simon & Schuster

Book design by Lani Cartier
Illustrations by Robin Nance

Menasha Ridge Press
Route 3   Box 450
Hillsborough, NC 27278
Distributed by Simon & Schuster

To
your four opponents
who didn't want me to write it!

Contents

Acknowledgments

I wish to acknowledge the following people, without whose help, this book never would have been written:

Fred Bonnie, for fostering my interest in writing;

Dede Self, for typing the manuscript and many revisions;

Jane, my wife, who made it possible;

Winston Churchill, when asked if he knew that he ended many of his sentences with a preposition, is reputed to have replied: "This is the sort of English up with which I will not put."

Disclaimer

No careful lawyer gives advice without qualifying it. After all, lawyers invented disclaimers, and here is mine.

This book is based on what I have seen happen to home buyers and existing laws. The facts of your particular case will differ, to some extent, from those I have related. In fact, I have never seen two cases with identical facts. Furthermore, some laws, especially the federal tax laws, may change and affect what I have said.

Another problem arises out of the fact that real estate laws, customs and practices vary to some degree throughout the country. This made it more difficult to cover all of the local variations.

For the foregoing reasons, I recommend that you consult with your legal or real estate representative.

Preface

During the early years of my law practice, before I became a real estate broker, I closed hundreds of real estate transactions for buyers and sellers of traditional and condominium homes. In my role as a closing attorney, it did not take me long to see that the buyers were led to believe that they were being protected or represented in what was, for most of them, the largest, single financial transaction of their lives.

Although many good books have been written about the nuts and bolts of home buying, I have not read one that talks about the deadly serious "sheep-shearing" game that is played behind the scenes for your money, or how to deal with it. There will be many "wolves in sheep's clothing" lurking in the bushes when you go out to buy your home. In the following pages I have done my best to teach you how to play their game without you losing your skin.

Some readers may bristle at what is presented. Those who do are probably one of your four wily opponents described in the following chapters.

HOME BUYERS

Lambs to the Slaughter?

Introduction:
Four Royal Fleecings

I have found that examples explain better than anything else. Therefore, I would like to begin with four cases that happened to buyers I represented. I will refer to these cases over and over again in later chapters to make various points about the home buying process. So, it might be a good idea for you to thoroughly familiarize yourself with these stories before proceeding to the next chapter.

The First Fleecing

A young woman, I will call her Nancy, came to see me about a problem she was having with her recently purchased home. It seems her basement was leaking, not only through her foundation, but as a result of her septic system backing up. The repair estimate was over $5,000. After talking with her for three hours (she was fairly hysterical) and visiting her neighbors, I developed the following about what had happened.

Nancy had been transferred to Birmingham by her company. When she learned she was being transferred, she flew to Birmingham to locate a home. She chose an agent of a real estate firm which had contacts with a real estate firm in her hometown.

After two full days of looking at houses, eating hamburgers in the front seat of the agent's car, discussing financing options, and so on, her agent located a house she liked, except for water stains in the basement. He called the sellers' agent about it and was told that squirrels had nested in a drain, clogging it up, but that the drain had since been cleaned out and the water problem solved.

Satisfied, Nancy negotiated a contract with the sellers contingent on her getting a Federal Housing Administration (FHA) loan. She applied for the loan, then flew home to prepare for the move.

The FHA inspector passed the home, and Nancy's credit and loan application were approved. On learning this, she flew back to Birmingham. The closing was set the next afternoon, and she was to return home following the closing.

On the morning of closing, Nancy made one last tour of the house, only to find water standing in several parts of the basement. She asked the sellers about it, and they said that the water had been blown through an open door during a recent thunderstorm. Nancy did not believe this but went to the closing with her agent. There waiting on them were the sellers' agent and a lawyer who was to handle the closing. The sellers, Nancy was told, had signed the papers earlier and would not be back.

Nancy, really suspicious by now, stated that she would not close until she had some straight answers about the water in the basement. In fact, she requested that another inspector look at it. Her agent told her there was not time to do it that day and reminded her that her airplane was leaving that evening. Nancy then said that she would close if all of the money was held until the cause of the water was determined. The sellers' agent said the sellers would never agree to that and that it was not necessary to hold back any money since the sellers had given their word and the FHA would stand behind the inspection. Nancy held her ground, and, along about this time, her agent started saying things to her clearly intending to make her feel guilty about not closing.

The lawyer then took Nancy into another room and told her that holding money back was not done in Birmingham because the buyer and seller too often got into a disagreement after the closing over who was entitled to it. Her advice to Nancy was to go ahead and close. But Nancy still held out.

Finally, both agents went to another room, then returned to announce that the sellers had agreed over the telephone to reduce the price of the home by $500, if Nancy would sign a release about the water problem. This, of course, did not satisfy Nancy, but the closing was wearing into its third hour; she was tired, outnumbered, and in danger of missing her flight. So, she closed and flew home. The first big rain brought her to my office.

I knew from an earlier sad case I had handled that the FHA did not have to stand behind its inspection, nor could the lender be made to pay, because Nancy did not hire the lender to make the inspection for *her*. But I felt that there probably was a good fraud case against the seller for lying and, possibly, the agents and lawyer for helping the sellers pull it off.

A talk to the neighbors confirmed the fraud. The sellers had been having water problems for as long as they owned the home. In all probability, the agents, or at least the sellers' agent, knew this. In addition, the sellers' agent was to make a commission on the home the sellers were buying—that deal being contingent on Nancy's closing. So the sellers' agent would lose doubly if Nancy backed out. Finally, the lawyer had been handling home closings for both agents for years and was to close the sellers' new home purchase. The lawyer knew that holding back the sales proceeds from Nancy's closing would delay the sellers closing on their next home and the agents getting their commissions.

With all of the lying and undercurrents going on, it was a great case for me. But it's still in progress, and Nancy's problem isn't resolved.

The Second Fleecing

In another case, a young divorcee, Jill, came to me with a water-in-the-basement problem, too. As you may have surmised, water is a major problem in my area. It may be something else in your area. A talk with the neighbors again revealed that the sellers knew of the water problem. But I also learned something else about the agent that I have not, until this day, had the heart to tell Jill.

Jill's ex-husband was required by their divorce decree to pay her a certain sum of money, with which to buy a home. She started looking for houses with a real estate agent who was a friend of the family. Nothing they saw suited Jill.

While out alone one day, Jill drove past a house with a For Sale By Owner sign in the front yard. She liked the outside appearance and called her agent friend to make arrangements to get inside.

The agent went to see the seller and told him she was working with a young divorcee whose ex-husband was buying her a home in the $115,000 price range. The agent then asked the seller what his price was and would he pay her a commission if she could get Jill to buy his home. The seller said, "Sure, I will pay a commission at that price."

The agent returned to Jill and they drew up an offer. A deal was struck at $113,000. Then the seller went around the neighborhood bragging about how he had netted $7,000 more than he was willing to take, because he knew what Jill was willing to pay. Jill's agent "friend" received a $6,780 commission, and since the seller netted $7,000 more than he had been willing to get, the price was inflated $13,780 ($6,780 + $7,000) by Jill calling her agent into the deal. And she had the water problem, too.

The Third Fleecing

In this case, a young couple, the Hopes, came to me about some problems they were having with their builder. It seemed he had bid too low on their home, and now, half-way through the job, he wanted to up the price or quit. If that wasn't bad enough, the home was being built on a lot the Hopes already owned, and they, not the builder, had borrowed the money from the bank to finance the costs of construction. On top of that, the builder had used some of the money the Hopes had given him for work and materials on other houses he was building, leaving several unpaid bills on the Hopes' home.

I didn't have to do any investigation to know that the builder was living hand-to-mouth and was not worth suing. I also knew that the cost of getting another builder to finish the work would be prohibitive. I worked it out by getting the builder to forego any profit and completing the home at his cost. But it still cost the Hopes an additional $9,000 to get their home completed and pay the builder's outstanding bills.

Then, after moving in, they found all sorts of little things that needed adjusting, as most buyers of newly-built homes do. After several broken promises to take care of it and, finally, a phone call from me, the builder came out, took care of about half of what needed to be done, and left. He wouldn't return our phone calls after that.

That summer, the Hopes noticed that their air conditioner wasn't cooling the home very well. A trip to the attic where the duct work was laid revealed that it had not been insulated as specified. When they called the builder this time, his telephone had been disconnected.

The Fourth Fleecing

The last fleecing involved the Wilts, who bought a home during a period of high interest rates. They couldn't afford the financing at that time, so the seller took back a $25,000 second mortgage for part of the purchase price. The mortgage provided that the Wilts were to pay it off within three years when it would "balloon." Their agent assured them that they would have no trouble doing this because their income would go up and interest rates would come down. This would allow them to refinance the first and second mortgage and pay off the sellers.

Three years went by and the Wilts were not able to arrange financing they could afford and came to me. I called the sellers to ask for more time, only to learn that the sellers had made a similar agreement on their home and needed the Wilts' money to pay off their loan.

I temporarily resolved the matter by getting the person the sellers owed to agree to extend the payoff time two years upon payment of $2,000. The sellers then made the same agreement with the Wilts, meaning the Wilts paid the $2,000, as well as my fee.

             *   *   *   *   *

These cases are typical of those I am asked to handle. Although not every home buyer gets fleeced like this, many do. There are many more times when less traumatic mistakes occur, and it's easier for the home buyer to just write it off to experience and get on with life. The sad thing is, most of these bad experiences, large or small, can be prevented. But before looking at how to avoid the shearers, lets analyze home buying.

Part 1

The Game
and Its Players

1 *An Overview of the Game*

As in the cases just mentioned, the first I usually hear about my clients buying a home is when they call me because the basement is full of water, they have just found massive termite damage, it's fifteen degrees outside and the furnace isn't working, or some other awful thing has happened. There is little I can say to them to make them feel better.

Sometimes, I get a call from clients who are trying to be careful, saying that they have just agreed to buy a home and that they want me to represent them. Well, if they have already made the agreement, what more is there, I wonder, for me to do? Before I started representing home buyers full time, I could count on my fingers the number of people who had come to me first, so that I could help them *prepare* to buy a home.

Emotions will blind you. The beginning, not the middle or end, determines how most investments turn out. Yet buying a home is such an emotional event for most people that they are unable to treat it as the truly significant investment that it is. Rather, they can only think about things like: where the baby's room will be, what color they will paint the living room, how beautiful the flower garden is in the back yard, how proud their parents will be when they see the home, or, like Nancy, making a return flight.

Ignorance and nonassertiveness are costly. In addition, most home buyers are so unfamiliar with the legal and factual aspects of buying a home and the potential dangers involved, that they lack the confidence needed to be assertive or to protect themselves, even when the need to do so has become crystal clear. For instance, many are reluctant to engage in tough price bargaining and often pay more, like Jill, than the seller would have taken. Or, like Nancy, they forego a thorough professional inspection, because the seller or real estate agent assures them that "it's a good home" or "it's been fixed."

Like lambs to the slaughter. So, like the proverbial "lambs to the slaughter," most home buyers let themselves be swept up in the frenzy of the home search and herded along by the other people involved, whose interests are adverse to their own. Then, after the closing, when it's too late to really alter what has happened without a lawsuit, any hidden dangers that were lurking in the closets give an unexpected and unhospitable house-warming party. This is when the feeling of having been fleeced sets in, and it is a feeling that, in most cases, can be avoided.

The real dangers. Contrary to popular belief, *people* problems, not title problems, will be your main dangers. You will be able to eliminate title problems by requiring that the seller furnish a warranty deed, marketable title, title insurance and a survey (which are fully discussed later). But none of those will protect you from your own ignorance or weakness as a negotiator, or someone else's dishonesty or greed.

Your opponents. You know what your weaknesses are, and I am going to give you some ideas that should help you deal with them. I am also going to tell you many important things about buying a home that you will not otherwise find out about until it is too late. But the first step in preparing to play the game is, I think, knowing who your opponents will be.

There are four wily opponents whom you are likely to face when you buy your home. They are (1) the seller, (2) the real estate agent, (3) the lender, and (4) the closing agent. They will be your opponents because they will all be playing for *your money*. If they don't get it, then they will have to try to get it from someone else, which means that they will have to start the game all over again. For this reason, they will be doing everything they can to get you to sign on the dotted line and to close. They will be less than pleased if you don't— remember this when one of them tries to give you advice.

*   *   *   *   *

Since a friendly real estate agent is the first opponent you will probably face and often the most dominant person in the transaction, let's drag her out of the bushes first.

2　*The Real Estate Agent*

All real estate agents must work under the supervision of a real estate broker. Both are licensed under state licensing laws, which are enforced by state commissions or licensing boards.

To become an agent, you must attend a real estate school approved by the state commission or licensing board and pass an examination. Broker requirements are more strenuous. When I went to the real estate agent's school, the instructor told the class in the first meeting that the purpose of the course was to teach us how to pass the examination. And I assure you little else was taught. Brokers around the country have told me this is also true of their schools.

Realtor®. Often people use the word Realtor® when referring to an agent or broker. A Realtor® is an agent or broker who is a member of an organization known as the National Association of Realtors® (NRA). Realtors® claim to be better trained and more ethical than non-Realtors®. And perhaps they are, but the agents in the four fleecings were Realtors®.

Commissions. Commissions earned on sales are divided between the agent making the sale and the broker. The split usually runs from 50/50 to 70/30 in favor of the agent. If two agents from the same firm work a deal, one has the seller and the other the buyer, they "co-op" (split) the agent portion of the commission. If two separate real estate firms work a deal, one having the seller and the other the buyer, the firms co-op the commission, then pay the agents their allotted shares. Co-oping is a common practice and leads to what I feel are grave abuses. I will explain what I mean a little later, but, first let's look at the responsibilities of agents and their brokers.

The rules. Under the law of agency, a real estate agent owes allegiance to his or her employer—the person who pays the agent's commission. In a residential real estate transaction, the agent's employer is almost always the seller. Few real estate agents will represent a buyer for hire. Those that will are discussed in a later chapter entitled "Your Own Representative."

So assuming the usual situation where the agent is paid by the seller, what are the agent's responsibilities in the transaction? In brief, the agent is duty bound to get the seller the best possible deal. This is because the law imposes a fiduciary duty on the agent to protect the interests of his or her employer, which is the highest duty of protection imposed by the law. In fact, it is similar to the duty of protection that a lawyer owes a client. You would not rely on the seller's lawyer to protect your interests, and you cannot rely on the seller's real estate agent to do it either.

How this affects you. You must recognize up front that most of the good things that an agent will tell you about a home should be disregarded. Agents, as salespeople, are entitled to use sales puffery, and they do. Statements like, "It's a great house," or "It's a super buy," mean nothing. If you do not believe me, ask an agent who says such things to put them in writing, but do not hold your breath waiting for it to happen. You can bet your last dollar that Nancy's agent would not have promised in writing that the basement would not leak. The only thing you will be likely to get in writing from an agent about the home is a release to sign at the closing saying that the agent did not misrepresent anything about the home to you and is not responsible for its condition. This, unfortunately, is when many home buyers first get an inkling of whom the agent really represents.

Agents are bound to tell the truth. Agents are required by law to be truthful with regard to any questions that you may have about the home and, in most states, must disclose to you any major defects in the home that they know exist. In other words, if an agent knows the basement leaks, then he or she is supposed to tell you about it.

Unfortunately, not all agents (like the sellers' agent in Nancy's case) are honest, and no reliable way has been invented to determine which ones are and which ones are not. Furthermore, an agent may not know that the basement leaks, and something that many home buyers do not know is that an agent is not required to inspect the home for you, assist you in the contract negotiations, or do anything else that might weaken the seller in the transaction. In fact, without the seller's prior approval, such acts would be a breach of the fiduciary duty that the agent owes the seller. For breaching that duty, an agent can lose any claim to a commission, be sued by the seller, and be disciplined by the state real estate regulatory agency, which partially explains the behavior of the agents in the cases of Nancy and Jill.

The agent's eternal conflict of interest. The other and more serious problem with agents is that, as salespeople, they do not get paid unless the deal closes. This, as demonstrated by my clients' misfortunes, can cause you a great deal of harm because it tends to make agents more interested in the closing than what's best for you. In an effort to get paid, agents will attempt to gain your trust, i.e., drive you in their car to see various homes, buy your lunch at McDonald's, talk about your family, tell you how cute your children are and promise to get you the best financing available. They may also tell you things about the seller they shouldn't—straddle the fence, in other words. Then they can play you and the seller against each other—telling the Wilts and their sellers that holding paper with a balloon was a good idea. They take a risk in doing this, though. The old biblical phrase, "No man can serve two masters," is steadfastly observed by the law. If an agent straddles the fence, he or she will end up as an illegal "double agent" with the conflicting duties of allegiance that naturally follow. Neither buyer nor seller can trust a double agent.

Co-oping compounds the deception. Although it can happen, as in Jill's case, when there is only one agent involved, the double agent situation most often arises when there are two agents, as in Nancy's case. They can work for different real estate firms or the same firm—it doesn't matter. As previously stated, this is called a co-op arrangement: the seller's agent (the listing agent) agrees to split the commission with another agent (the co-op agent), who furnishes the buyer. Both agents are the seller's agents by agreement, although the co-op agent usually misleadingly acts like he or she is representing just the buyer. When this occurs, the co-op agent is an illegal double agent. The co-op agent is never your agent in your dealings with the seller, as Nancy discovered to her rue.

The Federal Trade Commission's view. The Federal Trade Commission (FTC) completed a study of the real estate industry in 1981, which, at this writing, has not been published. A lot of people think the results of the study have been suppressed by powerful political forces. However, I was fortunate enough to obtain a copy of the staff report, a summary of the main study. Let me quote a pertinent passage from it:

> Most consumers assume their brokers provide them with sound advice and represent them in key aspects of the transaction. However, in the present . . . system of brokerage, buyers are without formal representatives. . . . The ambiguities and conflicts in a broker's role lead to false consumer expectations of representation and to potential and real abuse of the broker's fiduciary duties. These abuses include self-serving advice and steering, violation of consumer confidences, and others.

No wonder the main study hasn't been released!

The sign of an ethical agent. An ethical agent, whether or not a Realtor®, should say something like this to you up front:

> I want you to understand that I represent the seller, who pays me, and I cannot do anything for you that would hurt a seller. I will carry any offer you wish to make to the seller but cannot negotiate for you against the seller. If you feel you need help during the negotiations, then you should get someone else to advise you. However, I will do my best to help you find a home and financing that suit you.

It is rare to hear words like these, though.

Ways the seller's agent can help you. Nevertheless, you can use a seller's real estate agent or agents to your advantage in many areas of the transaction. For instance, they will know which homes are for sale, although they generally will show you homes that are listed with a real estate firm. This means you probably will not be seeing any For Sale By Owner homes.

If your agent's firm is a member of the National Association of Realtors®, it will have access to the Multiple Listing Service (MLS), a publication Realtors® put out which lists the homes that are for sale in a given area. In most areas only Realtors® have access to this publication, and it enables them to know about more homes being on the market in any given area.

MLS does have two drawbacks, though. First, there are no For Sale By Owner homes in it. Second, agents tend to show or favor homes that their firms have listed, which eliminates co-oping the commission with another firm. This hurts you because it restricts the MLS homes an agent will show you. Not all agents are this way, but many are and will try to show you only homes their firms have listed in MLS.

There are many other areas where real estate agents can help you. They can tell you approximately what your closing costs will be (they are required to do this before you sign anything in many states), and they will know what financing is available, the names of reputable home inspectors, interior decorators, contractors, insurers, attorneys and so on. Just make sure that any of these suggestions made by agents are price and quality competitive. Often, they will have a tying arrangement with the agent (they are friends or relatives and send business back and forth to each other) and may not feel pressured to be price competitive or even be competent.

Real estate agents can also be invaluable sources of information about the neighborhood conditions, schools, shopping areas, public transportation, fire and police protection and so forth. But, most important, many agents will give you useful information about the seller (although they are not supposed to do it without the seller's permission) that will aid you in the contract negotiations that will occur between you and the seller. For example, they often say that the seller will take less than the asking price, or has bought another home and must sell in a hurry, or other similarly compromising statements that give away the seller's weaknesses. They will tell the seller about your weaknesses, too, if you give them away, which is what happened to Jill.

*   *   *   *   *

I will come back to the real estate agent several more times as we work our way through the problems you can encounter buying a home. But first let's drag your other opponents out of the bushes and onto the playing field.

3 The Seller

How about the seller? Under the ancient legal rule of caveat emptor (Latin words meaning "let the buyer beware"), a purchaser of real estate, including a home, took the property "as is," unless the contract of purchase provided otherwise. Over the years, the courts in many states have relaxed this rule in certain areas.

What the seller must tell you. The seller of a used or existing home must now disclose any *hidden* and *dangerous* defects that he or she *knows* about (rotten floor joists and subflooring that the seller knows are in danger of collapsing); the seller cannot cover up defects to prevent you from seeing them (painting over water damaged areas on a ceiling that would give away a roof leak); and, if you ask any questions about the home, the seller is supposed to answer them truthfully.

Regardless of how caveat emptor has been modified, it can still hurt you. For instance, if you are buying a used home, who decides what is a hidden or dangerous defect? Leaking basements (as in Nancy's and Jill's cases) or roofs are annoying and can cost a lot of money to repair, but are they hidden or dangerous? How do you prove that a seller knew about a truly dangerous condition, such as rotten floor joists and subflooring or exposed wiring in the attic? And what about dangerous defects that a seller had no way to know existed, such as wooden support columns that had been hollowed out by termites or exposed wiring inside a wall? Then, there is the problem of dishonest sellers, like Jill's and Nancy's, who will not tell you that the roof leaks, or volunteer that the school district is being changed, even if you ask.

Protection for newly-built homes. In the area of newly-built homes, building codes offer substantial protection against the use of substandard materials and methods. In addition, the courts of many states have made consumer protection decisions that give a buyer of a newly-built home limited guarantees concerning the quality and fitness of construction of the home.

Pitfalls. However, buying a newly-built home does not eliminate all of the caveat emptor problems either. The new home guarantees created by the courts do not cover everything that might go wrong with a newly-built home. In general, these guarantees cover major problems, such as shifting foundations, water seepage into the living areas of the home, a septic system that does not work, and so forth—things that will seriously affect safety or the use and enjoyment of a home. Leaking windows, buckling siding, cracked driveways, standing water in the yard that could have been eliminated by proper landscaping, and so on are not always covered by the consumer protection guarantees, nor is the unfinished work such as the Hopes found upon moving in.

Furthermore, builders often get home buyers to close before all of the work is done; then it seems impossible to get them to return to finish the job. Or, they go broke and cannot finish or pay all of their suppliers, who file liens against the home. Consumer protection guarantees are obviously of little value against these problems, or when a builder like the Hopes', is no longer in business.

Precautions. Because of the various kinds of bad things that can happen to you, whether or not intended by the seller (meaning, also, a builder), it is very important that you do all that you can to protect yourself *before* paying any money or signing anything. Preliminary investigation, a good, protective contract of purchase (the sales contract), and constant vigilance are basic requirements.

You had better check out everything you can before signing the contract, which casts the die for the entire transaction and is the most important document for you. Unfortunately, it is usually drawn up by the buyer and the seller one evening at the seller's home, or by a real estate agent who represents the seller. I seldom see contracts of purchase—even those drawn by lawyers—that really protect a home buyer. Even after doing these things, you must resolve to never let down your guard. You can get blind-sided when you least expect it, like Jill.

*   *   *   *   *

I will discuss what to do to protect yourself in more detail later, but let's talk next about the financial opponents that you might be playing against.

4   *The Money Lenders*

Most would-be home buyers do not have enough cash lying around to buy a home outright, so they plan to borrow a major part of the purchase price. This arrangement is usually called a "mortgage" or, in some states, a "deed of trust." Under either arrangement, you put up the home as collateral for the loan. For the sake of simplicity, I will refer to such loans as mortgages.

You might get the seller to lend the money for part of the purchase price, which sometimes can be a good arrangement, but most sellers want cash or a very fast pay back that you (like the Wilts) cannot afford. In this case, you will have to go to someone who is in the business of lending money to home buyers, such as a mortgage banker, a savings and loan association, a bank and so forth.

The lender's inspection and appraisal. Before going into the details of financing, let's first look at something all commercial lenders do, which may cause you a lot of unexpected grief (as it did in Nancy's case). The lender will inspect and appraise the home before making a loan to you, but you cannot rely on the lender's inspection or appraisal to protect you. If you are getting a government related loan, such as those insured by the FHA or guaranteed by the Veterans

Administration (VA), you should be aware that neither of these are liable for faulty appraisals or inspections.

The lender's inspection and appraisal are made from a different viewpoint than yours; the lender only wants to know that it will be able to get its money back if it has to foreclose. Whereas, you want to know that the home is worth what you are paying for it. Furthermore, the lender knows that you will have to continue paying the loan back, even if the home falls down after you buy it and even if the lender's inspector *should* have discovered whatever caused it to fall down!

I have seen many cases of homes that never should have passed the lender's inspection, and appraisals, by strange coincidence, almost always come back at the agreed purchase price. This isn't all that shocking when you consider that inspectors and appraisers wouldn't make very good livings if they went around killing deals. You go to a commercial lender to get a loan, nothing more, which Nancy sadly learned.

Ways of borrowing money. Now let's look at ways to borrow money. Apart from borrowing from friends or relatives, you can borrow from a commercial lender such as a bank, savings and loan association, mortgage banker, the Federal Land Bank, to name a few, or the seller. When the seller lends you the money, it is called "holding paper" or a "seller's mortgage." I will refer to it as holding paper.

What follows next are several examples which explain the basics and which, along with the other things to follow, should enable you to play your lending opponents a better match. Unless otherwise indicated, assume that the price of the home is $80,000 and no closing costs or real estate commission are to be paid.

If you get a 75 percent commercial loan, then you will borrow $60,000 (.75 × $80,000). The balance, $20,000, is called the down payment. Most commercial lenders will require that the down payment come from savings and not be borrowed. You pay the proceeds from the loan and your down payment to the seller, who then pays off any mortgages against the home and pockets the difference.

If permitted by the lender, you could get the seller to agree to hold paper (a second mortgage, or simply a "second") for $10,000, which would reduce your cash requirement to $10,000.

If, instead, you are borrowing only from the seller, you could get the seller to hold paper (a first mortgage or simply a "first") for $60,000 and make a $20,000 down payment.

If the seller will hold paper and has a mortgage against the home, then the question of paying off the mortgage will arise. If the mortgage is for $15,000, then, in the previous example, the seller could pay it off and still have $5,000 left.

But, if the seller's mortgage is more than $20,000, $50,000 for example, then the seller will not get enough cash from you to pay off the mortgage. In this case, you could discuss taking over the seller's mortgage and buying the seller's "equity," the difference between the sales price and the existing mortgage, or $30,000 ($80,000 - $50,000). This type of transaction is called an "equity sale," and there are three ways you could do it:

(1) You could pay the seller $30,000 in cash and take over the existing first.

(2) Suppose you only have $20,000, then you could give the seller a second for $10,000, $20,000 cash and take over the first.

(3) Assuming again that you have only $20,000, you could give the seller another kind of second, called a "wraparound," for $60,000 and $20,000 cash. The seller will remain liable for and continue paying the first with money you pay on the second. The payments of the second should exceed those on the first for this to work. Wraparounds are one of the "creative financing" vehicles. The one demonstrated is a very simple

version. They are usually more complicated and can be dangerous. You shouldn't agree to one without consulting a real estate lawyer.

What is a mortgage? Now, let's look at features of mortgages. A mortgage really consists of two documents, a note, which is your promise to pay back the money, and a mortgage, whereby you pledge your home as security for the note. If you don't pay the note, the lender can either sue you for what you owe or foreclose. If you are foreclosed, you will have, in most states, the right to buy the property back for cash for a certain period of time. This right is called the "right of redemption."

What happens in an equity sale? When you take over a mortgage, you, in real estate jargon, either "assume" or "take subject to" it. When you assume a mortgage, you become personally liable to pay it. When you take subject to it, you are not personally liable to pay it. Otherwise, the two transactions are the same. In most equity sales, the buyer assumes the seller's mortgages—there can be more than one mortgage assumed or taken subject to. In a wraparound equity sale, the buyer takes subject to the seller's mortgage(s), which the seller continues to pay.

One other form of seller financing. Another way the seller can loan you the purchase price is when the seller retains title until you pay the full purchase price. This is called by various names in different areas: lease/purchase, contract for a deed, bond for title, installment sales contract and land sales contract. If you cannot make all of the payments, the owner can treat you like a mere tenant and evict you, no foreclosure necessary. Furthermore, if the seller dies, gets divorced, goes insane, becomes senile or goes bankrupt before you get your deed, then you will be tied up in a court proceeding.

These types of arrangements are often used in cases where a buyer cannot make a down payment—a no-money-down deal. Avoid them, if you can. However, if you end up in one of these deals, record the contract of purchase just as you would a deed. This step puts the whole world on notice of your agreement with the seller and prevents the seller from selling the home to someone else and cutting you off.

Financing features. There are certain features which will affect how much you pay and when you pay that are discussed in the following paragraphs:

The **interest rate** is the cost of the money you are borrowing. For instance, if you borrow $1,000 at 10 percent interest, after one year you will owe $100 in interest (.10 × $1,000) as well as the $1,000.

The higher the interest rate, the larger your payments will be. For instance, on a $60,000, thirty-year loan, your monthly payments at 10 percent interest would be $526.80, but would be $617.40 with a 12 percent interest rate.

And the bigger your loan is, the higher your payments will be. For example, the payments on a $70,000, thirty-year loan at 12 percent interest would be $720.30.

These calculations can be made using a factor table, like the one that follows, which you can obtain from many lending institutions or commercial office supply companies. There are also calculators on the market that are programmed to compute mortgage payments.

The Factor Table allows you to calculate your monthly mortgage payments for the interest rates and loan terms given. You do it by multiplying .001 × the loan factor × the loan amount. For instance, to compute the monthly mortgage payment on a $70,000, thirty-year, 12 percent loan, the loan

Factor Table

Interest rate	15 years	20 years	25 years	30 years
9 %	$10.15	$ 9.00	$ 8.40	$ 8.05
9¼	10.30	9.16	8.57	8.23
9½	10.45	9.33	8.74	8.41
9¾	10.60	9.49	8.92	8.60
10	10.75	9.66	9.09	8.78
10¼	10.90	9.82	9.27	8.97
10½	11.06	9.99	9.45	9.15
10¾	11.21	10.16	9.63	9.34
11	11.37	10.33	9.81	9.53
11¼	11.53	10.50	9.99	9.72
11½	11.69	10.67	10.17	9.91
11¾	11.85	10.84	10.35	10.10
12	12.01	11.02	10.54	10.29
12¼	12.17	11.19	10.72	10.48
12½	12.33	11.37	10.91	10.68
12¾	12.49	11.54	11.10	10.87
13	12.66	11.72	11.28	11.07
13¼	12.82	11.90	11.47	11.26
13½	12.99	12.08	11.66	11.46
13¾	13.15	12.26	11.85	11.66
14	13.32	12.44	12.04	11.85
14¼	13.49	12.62	12.23	12.05

factor is $10.29 and the equation is .001 × $10.29 × $70,000 = $720.30.

The interest rate you pay will be affected by what money costs your lender, alternative investment vehicles, and the following described features. Throughout this discussion, keep in mind that you probably will be able to get a lower rate of interest from the seller holding paper than you will from a commercial lender.

The **loan term** is the length of time you will have to pay back (amortize) the loan. The most popular term for many years has been thirty years. But lenders will often give you a lower interest rate on a shorter term because the risk of the lender being exposed to a long and unpredictable period of higher interest rates is reduced.

Often the loan term is artificially shortened with what is called a balloon payment. For example, a loan is set up on a regular basis for thirty years, but is all due and payable in five years. This is another type of creative financing and like most balloons, tends to "pop." The Wilts' loan is one of these.

The loan term will also affect your monthly payments, as well as the total you will pay over the life of the loan. For instance, on a $60,000, thirty-year loan at 12 percent interest, the monthly payments are $617.17, whereas they are $720.30 on a similar fifteen-year loan. So the shorter term loan costs more per month. On the other hand, on the fifteen-year loan, you will pay a total of $129,654 ($720.30 × 12 months × 15 years), but on the thirty-year loan your total payments will be $222,264 ($617.40 × 12 months × 30 years). The difference is all interest.

Before you leap into a fifteen-year loan, though, look at the break-even point, i.e., when the thirty-year loan starts costing you more than the fifteen-year one. This occurs during the eighteenth year of this particular example. Only after then, would the fifteen-year mortgage cost you less overall. So, unless you plan to live in this house at least eighteen years, you will not come out ahead with the shorter mortgage. Most people live in a home an average of about seven years, in case you're wondering about the odds of your staying that long. This analysis does not take into consideration after-tax computations, which would not significantly affect the result.

Points, as they are called, are closing costs which are expressed as a percentage of the loan amount; one point on a $60,000 loan is $600 (.01 × $60,000). Points come in two forms, discount points and loan fees (or origination fees). Each runs from one to several percent of the loan. Discount points are tax deductible by the buyer (borrower), but not by the seller. Loan fees are not tax deductible. However, I have seen many cases where a deduction was taken for loan fees.

In other cases, the lender has agreed in advance to classify loan fees as discount points. This enables the buyer to obtain a larger tax deduction. In any event, pay the points by separate check at closing, which is required by the Internal Revenue Service.

Discount points are charged by a commercial lender to get a higher effective interest rate on your loan than that stated in the loan documents. For instance, if you borrow $60,000 and pay two discount points, or $1,200 (.02 × $60,000), this is really borrowing only $58,800 but paying interest on $60,000. Loan fees, on the other hand, are charged by a commercial lender, supposedly to cover the costs of originating the loan. Both types of points vary from lender to lender and can be negotiated. Sellers holding paper usually do not charge points of any kind.

Loans carrying a large number of points usually have a lower interest rate than loans with few points. A high number of points are what have historically been used to keep the interest rates on FHA, VA and Federal Land Bank loans artificially below market interest rates. The Federal Land Bank has a sneaky way of charging points that a few other lenders use, too. It's called "share collateral." Here's how it works.

They get you to sign a note for $60,000, but only give you $58,800. The $1,200 is held by them as share collateral until you pay back the balance. As you can see, there's no difference in this and paying a two-point discount. The sharing is all done by you. Oh, yes, they loan your $1,200 out to someone else at interest.

Variable rate loans are usually made by commercial lenders, although I have seen sellers holding paper with a variable interest rate. The interest rate for this type of loan fluctuates with market interest rates, up or down (usually up, it seems). Most variable rate loans provide for periodic adjustments in the interest rate to stay in line with market rates. The monthly payments are also adjusted from time to time to reflect changes in the loan rate of interest.

Often there is a limit, called a cap, on how much the monthly payment can be raised or lowered in any specified period of time, for example, ten percent in any one year. When there is a cap and interest rates rise more than the monthly payments are allowed by the cap to rise, you will not be able to pay all of the interest and the loan will grow larger instead of the usual smaller. This is what is called "negative amortization."

Because there is little risk of loss if market interest rates go up, the lender will make a variable rate loan at a lower rate of interest and with fewer points. Variable rate loans also tend to have fewer resale restrictions. All of this is good for you. But you will suffer a slow, agonizing death if rates go up and stay up.

Graduated payment loans are loans where the payments start off lower than normal, gradually increase over a period of time, then level off for the remainder of the loan term. The leveling off point is usually five years. The amount you save in the early years is usually added to the loan balance. The idea here is to allow someone with low income but with higher income potential to buy now and pay more later when income goes up. Graduated payment loans are usually made by commercial lenders—rarely by sellers.

A **buy-down loan** is where the seller (usually the builder) pays the lender additional points at the closing to give you either an initially or a permanently lower interest rate. The cost to you is usually a higher price for the home. This is one situation where the lender's appraisal is almost always too high.

Subsidized loans are ones like the popular FHA and VA, as well as those targeted to help low income people buy homes or encourage urban renewal. Often these loans have graduated payment or buy-down features. The subsidies take various forms, such as guarantees against default (reducing the lender's risk of nonpayment), cash grants and tax exempt loans. The latter encourage a lender because the interest received is tax free. Subsidized loans usually carry a below market rate of interest, a little or no down payment and are almost exclusively made by commercial lenders.

Sales restrictions are designed to make you very unhappy when you least expect it. I remember a client who learned at the closing of the sale of her home that she was going to have to pay $1,200 prepayment penalty for paying her loan off early.

Prepayment penalties give the lender the right to charge you points for paying off your loan early. The usual purpose of these things is to prevent you from refinancing or otherwise paying off your loan during periods of lower interest rates. Prepayment penalties do not affect you when you buy a home, but they surely can affect you when you sell one.

FHA and VA loans do not have prepayment penalties. Any other loan will have one of these buggers, unless the note says that you can prepay it without penalty. The reason for this is that the lender is normally entitled to refuse prepayment, unless it includes all of the interest that the lender would have earned over the life of the loan. I suspect that many lawyers would be surprised to learn of this.

Another little fiendish device is the "alienation" clause (it almost hurts to say the word). Lenders use alienation clauses to prevent a homeowner from passing on a fixed rate conventional low interest loan to a buyer during periods of high interest rates. Alienation clauses come in two basic varieties (both bad) and colors (black and blue), and either can kill an equity sale, now or later when you go to sell. These clauses will be in either the note, mortgage or both. If, after what follows, you are not sure what to look for, ask the lender if there is one.

The first variation is the "due-on-sale" clause. Very simply, this clause says that the lender has the unfettered right to call the loan when the home is sold. Often, a lender having a due-on-sale clause mortgage will allow an equity sale (not out of compassion, though) by treating it like the other kind of alienation clause, commonly known as "Paragraph 17," (the number of the paragraph of the form mortgage that made this device infamous back in the 1970s).

Paragraph 17 clauses say that, on an equity sale, the lender has the right to check the purchaser's credit (which is reasonable), charge points (it gets worse) and raise the interest rate. This paragraph revolutionized the mortgage industry and it gets even worse.

The Federal National Mortgage Association, commonly known as Fannie Mae and which buys more Paragraph 17 loans than all other investors, decided in 1983 to treat Paragraph 17 as a due-on-sale clause. This policy was implemented for new as well as the existing Paragraph 17 mortgages, even though people owning homes with these mortgages on them were told when they bought their homes that these were "readjustable" mortages (i.e, the interest rate could be raised on an equity sale).

There was not a real estate lawyer, real estate agent or broker or lender in the United States who ever dreamed that Paragraph 17 mortgages were due-on-sale. In fact, the real estate lawyers I know feel that Paragraph 17 mortgages cannot legally be treated as being due-on-sale. And Fannie Mae has backed off its due-on-sale policy when pushed, so don't let it or any other lender "pull the wool over your eyes" on this one.

Now, not all loans have alienation clauses, FHA, VA and variable rate loans the chief ones that do not. If the loan is of another variety, you should check it for an alienation clause before signing anything. If you are getting a new loan, try to get the lender to promise you that your loan will not be sold to Fannie Mae after you close. If there is an alienation clause, or if the loan is going to be sold to Fannie Mae, you might be able to go another route, which would be better for you.

Applying to assume a loan. This will be required when there is an alienation clause, whether the commercial lender or seller holds the mortgage. The application procedures and computations are about the same as for applying for a new commercial loan, except that you probably will not be charged for an appraisal. You may have to pay at the closing for updating the lender's title insurance policy. Updating a title insurance policy is discussed later.

If there is an alienation clause, then you will be required to pay a point or two and a higher interest rate to take over the seller's mortgage. If you ever sell the home, the same thing will happen to your buyer.

Applying for a new commercial loan. Now, it's time to talk about applying for a new commercial loan, such as a conventional, VA, FHA or Federal Land Bank loan. The lender will want to see your contract of purchase and will ask you to fill out a credit application and pay money for a credit report and appraisal. These could run you $125 to $300, or more, depending on where you live. So, before giving the lender any money for these items, you should be satisfied that you know what the lender will give you in return and that you can afford it.

It's best to get a written commitment from the lender, stating the loan amount, term, interest rate and points for the loan you will receive. Most lenders restrict the time that the commitment will last, and many will not guarantee the in-

terest rate or points unless you pay a commitment fee, usually
one or two points, for which you get credit when you close.
Some lenders use applications that say you will owe a point or
two if you are approved for the loan but do not close.

Before you sign the loan application, the lender is required
to give you a statement of your estimated loan closing costs
(there may be other costs not related to the loan which will
not be on this estimate). After you have made the application,
the lender will begin checking your credit references, income
history, employment history, assets and liabilities, as well as
have the house appraised and, in some cases, inspected (for
the lender, not you).

Income guidelines. There are certain income guidelines
that vary from lender to lender, but it probably would be
safe to assume that, if your projected mortgage payments
(including taxes and insurance) do not exceed 30 percent of
your gross monthly income, you will meet these income guidelines.

In looking at your monthly payments, the lender will first
compute the payments to principal and interest, which on
a $60,000, thirty-year loan at 12 percent interest would be
$617.17. To that the lender will add one-twelfth of the esti-
mated annual taxes and homeowner's insurance premium. If
taxes will be $2,400 and the insurance premium $1,200, this
will bring the payments up by $300 ($2,400 + $1,200 divided
by 12) to $917.17. If the loan is FHA or a conventional loan for
more than 80 percent of the purchase price, then there will be
a small additional monthly charge for what is called "mortgage insurance." The proceeds of the mortgage insurance are
paid to the lender if it later has to foreclose your loan. As
stated before, all of these computations can be made using
a factor table or a calculator having loan amortization capa-
bilities.

Down payment guidelines. The down payment is, as previously explained, the cash portion of the purchase price which is not borrowed. The amount of the down payment is negotiable when the seller is to hold paper, but commercial lenders have fairly rigid guidelines for down payments. Simply stated, the down payment on a commercial lender's loan will be a certain percentage of the purchase price or the appraised value, *whichever is less.*

On most conventional loans (those other than FHA or VA), you can borrow up to 95 percent, paying only 5 percent down. But for any conventional loan over 80 percent, you will, as stated above, have to pay mortgage insurance, in addition to the mortgage payments, taxes and hazard insurance. The total dollar amount you can borrow on a conventional loan will vary from lender to lender.

On FHA loans, which are insured by the federal government, you can borrow 97 percent of the first $25,000 of the purchase price and 95 percent of the balance. For instance, on a $50,000 home, you can borrow $48,000 (.97 × $25,000 = $24,250 plus .95 × [$50,000 − $25,000] = $23,750). There is a ceiling, which varies around the country, on the dollar amount that you can borrow. FHA loans are geared to low to middle priced homes, but not the expensive models.

VA loans, on the other hand, are not insured but are "guaranteed" up to a certain amount. For several years, the maximum dollar guarantee has been $27,500. You usually can borrow up to four times the guarantee ($110,000) without making any down payment, assuming you meet the income guidelines and the home is appraised for that amount. You can obtain an even larger VA loan (in fact, there is no limit on the size VA loan you can get, assuming the other stated requirements are met), but you will have to make a downpayment to do it. The amount of the down payment will vary from lender to lender.

There are many different laws affording VA loan benefits, too many to attempt to present here. In general, you must have served in our armed forces. The only safe way to find out if you are entitled to one and how much the VA will guarantee for you is to call the Veterans Administration Regional Office in your area, and ask to speak to someone in the Loan Guaranty Processing Section of the Loan Guaranty Division.

Credit life insurance. Another form of insurance offered by lenders, but usually not required, is called "credit life insurance." This is decreasing term life insurance, which pays off your mortgage if you or your spouse die. If you want it, you can usually get it a lot cheaper somewhere else.

Shop around. There is competition among lenders, and you can get a lower interest rate here, fewer points there and so forth. A knowledgeable real estate agent or real estate lawyer will know who has what to offer in your area, but don't forget about tying arrangements. Agents and lawyers can have these with lenders, too. In any event, it will pay to shop around. Getting a loan is not very different from buying an automobile. You will usually get a better deal by comparing prices and playing lenders off against each other.

5   *The Closing Agent*

As you can see, buying a home can get pretty involved, and by now you may be feeling that you need someone to advise you. Well, you are not going to be able to rely on the closing agent (sometimes called the settlement or escrow agent). This is the opponent who closes the deal for everyone involved, i.e., you, the seller, the lender, the title insurance company, and, last but not least, the real estate agent(s). The closing agent will be a lawyer, title insurance company, commercial lender, or the seller's real estate firm. The last three will have their own lawyer review and/or prepare the closing documents.

What you can and cannot expect. The closing agent's job is to prepare all of the documents and to make sure that the title is in order, that the survey (if any) is clean, that the requirements of the mortgage lender and the title insurance company have been met, that all funds have been collected and properly disbursed and that the necessary documents have been recorded.

Although these services are important, they fall far short of protecting *you*. The closing agent is not responsible to you for anticipating problems, negotiating for you, drafting the contract of purchase, arranging your financing or making sure that the seller honors his or her agreement with you.

Another double agent. In other words, the closing agent does not represent you and is, at best, neutral. At worst, and in most cases, the closing agent has a tying arrangement (usually undisclosed) with either the real estate agent (which happened in Nancy's case) or with the mortgage company, both of which are on the other team. Because they send the closing agent a lot of business, the closing agent is very sensitive to the fact that, if you do not close, a client will be very unhappy (another version of the double agent). Furthermore, the closing agent's fee will not be paid unless you close —all the more reason for you not to rely on one. So, who can you rely on?

6   *Your Own Representative*

Most home buyers would probably benefit from hiring either their own lawyer or a buyer-paid real estate agent (but not both) as their representative. Although it is rare to find one, there are some real estate agents that represent buyers as well as sellers. Call your local Board of Realtors®, title insurance company or a real estate lawyer to find out if there are any in your area. If you can find one of these "enlightened" real estate agents, you might come out better than you would hiring your own lawyer. In fact, the entire home buying process would benefit from buyers being able to hire their own agent, rather than having to become involved with a traditional real estate agent.

Why pay an agent? In the first place, the commission the seller pays is padded into the price of the home, meaning you pay the commission of the seller's agent. In the second place, paying your own agent will make that agent your advocate. You become the principal, meaning that the agent's fiduciary duty is to protect your interests and not those of the seller. Thus, many of the disadvantages of working with the traditional real estate agent disappear. Furthermore, an agent you are paying will gladly show you For Sale By Owner homes, something traditional agents usually will not do. If Jill had been paying her agent, the agent could not legally have disclosed Jill's position to the owner, and there would have been some serious, as opposed to "friendly," negotiating.

An agent, accustomed to representing buyers for a fee, will probably know as much or more about buying a home than will most lawyers. Furthermore, such an agent will know which homes are for sale (especially if he or she is a Realtor® and has access to the Multiple Listing Service) and will show them to you. Lawyers will not know which homes are for sale, but, even if they do, can you imagine one taking the time to show them to you, or how much a lawyer would charge you for doing it?

Fee arrangements with buyer-paid agents. Buyer-paid real estate agents usually charge a percentage of the purchase price or a flat fee (usually one-half of a standard commission), if you buy, and most will charge you by the hour for consultation. Always bear in mind that the agent will not get paid under a percentage or flat fee arrangement unless you close, which will tend to make the agent more concerned about you closing than what is best for you. The percentage arrangement has a second disadvantage in that it penalizes your agent for getting you a better price.

It doesn't cost more. Having your own agent can result in an interesting development in your favor, if the seller also has an agent. Since you are paying your agent, the seller's agent will not have to co-op the commission paid by the seller with your agent. Therefore, the commission paid by the seller, and thus the price of the home, can be reduced by the amount of what the co-op commission would have been. The reduction in price will save you the commission you pay your own agent.

Let's look at an example of how this works on a $100,000 sales price with a $6,000 commission. The old way, you pay the seller $100,000, then the seller pays the agents $6,000, leaving the seller with $94,000. The new way, you pay the seller $97,000 and your agent $3,000 ($100,000 total), and the seller pays his or her agent $3,000, which again nets the seller $94,000. Agents who represent the buyer for a fee are accustomed to working out this kind of arrangement with a seller's agent.

If, like Jill, you are interested in a For Sale By Owner home, then you pay the agreed commission, 3 percent in this example, to your agent. Here's how Jill's case might have turned out for her with this arrangement.

Price actually paid	$ 113,000
Less commission actually paid	– 6,780
Price before commission was added on	$ 106,220
Less seller's windfall	– 7,000
Seller's taking price	99,220
Plus 3 percent commission (.03 × $99,220)	+ 2,976
Cost of home without the agent's "help"	$ 102,196

Of course, Jill's agent might have detected the water problem, or suggested a good home inspector who would have, or talked to the neighbors and discovered it on her own. Then Jill wouldn't have even bought the house!

Other listings of the agent or the agent's firm. There is one situation that you must look out for, though, if you plan to hire you own agent. The agent or the agent's firm will probably have listings to sell homes for various sellers in the area. If the agent tries to show one of these homes to you, there will be a conflict of interest—the double agent problem again. The agent or the agent's firm will be placed in the impossible position of trying to get both you and the seller the best possible deal. Therefore, you will have to either accept this situation or not look at homes that firm has listed for sale. In larger cities, there should be many homes for sale by other firms, but in small towns and rural areas this may not be the case. For this reason, buyer-paid real estate agents usually work in larger communities.

The NAR's view of buyer-paid agents. The National Association of Realtors® is squarely opposed to the buyer-paid agent idea. I have copies of letters, articles, talks and a legal brief by the NAR's general counsel and senior vice-president, Mr. William D. North, proving this fact. My feeling is that Mr. North and the more than 600,000 members of his organization do not want buyer representation because it would place home buying on an "at arm's length" basis, meaning agents would no longer be able to serve two masters in an effort to control the deal and get themselves paid. Deals negotiated at arm's length are harder to work out but they protect the buyers and sellers, not the agents.

The VA's view of buyer-paid agents. Most people think the VA is looking out for the veteran. Maybe. Quoting from "the horse's mouth" denying the right of VA loan applicants to pay their own agents:

> It is customary in the sale of residential property for the seller to list the property and pay the commission when a buyer is found. To allow otherwise would, in our opinion, lead to subterfuge and deception in an attempt to pass the cost on to veterans to their disadvantage.[1]

> Loan submissions in which it is contemplated that a real estate commission be paid by the veteran purchaser will be returned unprocessed, and sanctions may be con-

1. Portion of letter of 1/2/78 from J. R. Franks, Loan Guaranty Officer, Veterans Administration Regional Office, Washington, D.C.

sidered against any person(s) or entity(ies) found to be involved in any deliberate contravention of VA Regulation 4312 in this respect.[2]

This absurd position means you will not be able to use a buyer-paid agent if you are getting a VA loan—even though *you* pay the seller's real estate commission that has been added onto the price of the home!

VA and FHA foreclosures. There is a related problem if you find a VA or FHA foreclosure you wish to buy. Both VA and FHA regulations require that (a) the sale be conducted through a real estate firm and (b) a full commission be paid. This eliminates the possiblity of dealing direct and saving a commission. It also nixes the advantage of hiring your own agent to work for a half commission, since a full commission must be paid.

For instance, if the home is being sold for $80,000 and the built-in commission is $4,800 (6 percent), you can not get the price down to $75,200 ($80,000 – $4,800) on your own or hire your own agent on a 3 percent basis and get the price down to $77,600 ($80,000 – $2,400). And, no, your agent can not accept the full $4,800 commission and give you back $2,400 of it. That's an illegal rebate which could cost your agent his or her real estate license.

One wonders if there isn't some common cause behind the withholding of the FTC study, NAR's position on buyer-paid agents, the VA's buyer-paid agent policy, and the VA and FHA foreclosure policies. It seems that there is a very strong force (600,000 plus, strong) protecting the traditional co-oping system in all areas of residential real estate. This will not change, in my opinion, until buyers start demanding representation and an end to a system that promotes double deal-

2. Portion of letter from Mr. Franks of 1/12/78.

ing on all fronts. If you are interested in doing something about this, write your congressman and Who's Who in Creative Real Estate, 921 E. Main St., Suite F, Ventura, CA 93001, an organization of real estate people dedicated to eliminating co-oping and double agents.

Selecting a lawyer. If, instead, you decide to hire a lawyer to represent you, keep in mind the fact that few lawyers do any work in the home buying area. Your best bet will be to find one who is an experienced residential lawyer. You should be able to get a list of such lawyers from a banker, title insurance company, probate court or your own lawyer, but make sure that the lawyer you select does not have a tying arrangement with any real estate agent or agents that might become involved. And don't be afraid to ask! If there is a tying arrangement, the lawyer will have a conflict of interest between representing you and maintaining his or her relationship with the agent—the double agent problem again.

Don't scare the seller. If hiring a lawyer is not the usual way of doing things in your area, you may scare the seller to death by hiring one. If this is true where you live, use your lawyer as a silent partner, at least until the contract is signed. After that, there will be little that the seller can do to change things.

The lawyer's fee. You can expect to pay your lawyer several hundred dollars or more, depending on the time invested, the amount of money involved and the complexity of your particular transaction. If this seems like a lot of money, remember that if the seller is using a real estate agent, you are paying the agent's commission, because it is added onto the price of the home and the seller's agent does not even represent you! Also, your lawyer will probably be able to save you far more than the legal fee by negotiating effectively and drafting an offer of purchase that eliminates many of the problems that can arise after the closing.

Any lawyer should be willing to estimate in advance the amount of the fee, so you will be able to shop around to some degree. But keep in mind that a $75-per-hour lawyer may be able to work miracles compared to a $50-per-hour lawyer, and in less time. As with any other business transaction, you should withhold a generous part of your lawyer's fee until the matter is concluded. Whatever you do, though, never let your lawyer think that you will have trouble paying the fee. This, as you might imagine, will chill your lawyer's desire to represent you.

Avoid friends and relatives. If you decide to hire your own representative, whether a buyer-paid agent or lawyer, try to avoid a relative or close friend. Buying a home is so emotional that the last thing you will want is your brother-in-law or next-door neighbor telling you what to do, or, even worse, being afraid to do so. On the other hand, how do you fire relatives or friends if you don't like the kind of job that they are doing? And what if your friend turns out to be like Jill's agent? Many families and friendships have been fractured because of this.

When to hire a representative. Hire your representative *before* you do anything or talk to anyone else, especially any traditional real estate agents. You will need to plan your strategy and position yourself before you go house hunting, and your representative will be able to give you a lot of help there. If you wait until after you have made the agreement before you hire your representative, then about all he or she will be able to do for you is try to get you out of any holes that you have dug for yourself, a tough task in most cases.

Traditional agents will be upset. Many real estate agents with whom I have had dealings became quite upset when a prospective home buyer engaged their own representative. This might happen to you if you hire one—another good reason to use your representative as a silent partner. This is a natural reaction by the seller's agent. When the buyer has his or her own representative, the agent's job becomes harder; the agent now has to deal at arm's length (for a change) with someone who knows as much or more about the transaction as the agent.

In fact, I have known of many instances where an agent has told a would-be home buyer, who expressed an interest in getting help, that such action would not be necessary because there would be a lawyer at the closing. Having already had the pleasure of meeting the closing agent, you politely disregard this false assurance if it is given.

*   *   *   *   *

Prior to publication I showed the manuscript of this book to a closing attorney friend to get his comments. He said, "I really like your book, Sloan, and hope that you keep up the good work. People need to know about these things. But I hope you won't mind if I don't keep it out in my waiting room after it's published."

This anecdote is an example of how much real estate agents do not like for a buyer to have a representative. Of course, he knew that no real estate agent who saw it there would send him any more business—ever.

Part 2

Changing the Rules of the Game

Introduction: The Golden Rule

Regardless of whether or not you decide to hire your own representative, there are several things that you can do that will enable you to play the game better. The suggestions that follow are made in the general order of their occurrence in the home buying process. Depending on the facts of your case, some will be more important to you than others. Those of lesser importance often can be used as negotiating chips, to be shrewdly given up in return for concessions from the seller.

Your opponents will "howl" over some of my suggestions, because the game won't be nearly as much fun for them as it was. Expect to hear statements like, "This isn't the way this is usually done," "This could cause problems," or "The seller will never agree to this!" But don't let that scare you back into your sheepskin. The laws of most states and the rules of the National Association of Realtors® require that an agent present any offer you make to the seller, and, as long as you still have what your opponents want (your money and signature on the dotted line), you can change the rules of the game and have a chance of winning. This is a modified version of the Golden Rule which goes like this: "Those who have the gold make the rules." Now, the rule changes.

7   *Pregame Strategy*

When to buy. As a rule, you should buy in the fall or winter, which is when the residential market is usually the slowest and when you can obtain a better price. However, this may not apply where the weather is warm year round.

Sellers generally like to put their homes on the market when the weather is pretty, the flowers are up, and it is warm outside. This is when a home looks and feels its best. You, on the other hand, want to see it when it is at its worst, which is when it is cold, wet and dreary outside. That is when you have the best chance to find septic tank problems, water leaks, poor insulation, air infiltration and so forth.

You can probably assume that a seller, who is selling in the late fall or winter, has had the home on the market for several months and is discouraged, or has had something come up that is forcing him or her to sell at the seller's worst possible time of the year. Such a seller will be in a weaker position, which is what you want when you enter the contract negotiations.

Another thing to consider is the state of the real estate market where you live. If homes are moving quickly, you are in what is called a "seller's market." If homes are moving slowly, then you are in a "buyer's market." [1] High interest rates

1. 1983 was considered a buyer's market in most parts of the country. In Birmingham, only 31.46 percent of the homes listed for sale with a member of MLS actually sold, leaving a lot of desperate sellers out there. Your local Board of Realtors® probably has this information for your area, but it will be tough to get. An agent or broker who is a Realtor® can get it for you in many cases, though.

often accompany a buyer's market. You will probably be able to get a better price in a buyer's market and have a better chance to get a seller to hold paper. The seller holding paper will get you a lower interest rate and "after-the-closing" protection which is discussed later.

Sell existing home first. If you already own a home, you should consider selling it before contracting to buy your next home. There are two reasons for taking this approach.

First, if you enter into a contract to buy your next home before selling your existing home, you will be under pressure to sell your existing home in a hurry. This means you probably will not get as much for it as you would if you could be patient about selling it.

Second, most people cannot afford two homes. So, if you try to buy your next home first, you will have to make your offer of purchase contingent on selling your existing home. This is a very weak offer, and you will probably not be able to get the seller to negotiate the price, terms and so on to your liking. In fact, the seller may not even consider such an offer.

Even if such an offer is considered, the seller will insist on having the right to sell to someone else that might come along later, unless you then agree to remove the contingency regarding selling your existing home. This arrangement is called a "break clause," perhaps because of the number of nervous breakdowns it has caused. An example of such a break clause is:

> If Seller gets another offer acceptable to Seller, then Seller may accept said offer and cancel this contract, unless Buyer agrees to remove the contingency about first selling Buyer's home.

You are probably wondering where you will live if you sell first, buy last. I admit that this is an unsettling thought.

Possibly you can arrange to delay the closing or possession date on the home you are selling until the fall or winter, which will give you time to shop during the best buying months; maybe you have friends or relatives who will put you up for a while or know someone who needs a house sitter; maybe there is an apartment you can rent on a short-term basis. This might seem like a lot of bother and extra expense, however, the money you save selling then buying should more than repay you for it.

If you are nervous about not tying down your new home before selling your existing one, there is a sneaky alternative you might try: make your offer to buy the new one contingent on obtaining financing. The odds are great that no lender will make the loan until you have sold your existing home, which will get you the result you want. The problem with this approach is that most real estate agents are on to it, but you might find one who isn't or an unknowledgeable seller trying to sell without an agent.

One other negative about selling first, buying last, is that it will cost you your home loan interest deduction for tax purposes until you buy your next home. Your tax bracket and time out of ownership will be important factors to consider.

Out-of-towners. If you will be moving in from out of town, like Nancy, you will be what real estate agents call an "out-of-towner." Agents love to work with out-of-towners, who usually aren't in a position to spend a lot of time looking or negotiating for a home. To an agent, an out-of-towner is a quick sale—money in the bank.

Such time pressure will put you in an extremely weak bargaining position and could result in your paying too much for your new home, not to mention buying one that you later discover you do not really like.

If you will be an out-of-towner, you should consider leasing an apartment or house when you move to your new location, rather than buying a home. This will take away the time pressure and give you the breathing room that you will need to find a home that you really like and to properly negotiate for it. The extra moving or storage costs that you incur will be more than repaid by the cost savings and finding a home that is right for you.

I made this suggestion to the relocation executive of a major corporation headquartered in Birmingham, which moves over 1,000 employees a year. His reaction was very negative. "We don't want our employees wasting time looking for a home; we want them to get to work!" he said. I later found out his company had a sweetheart deal with a major relocation company, which, in turn, had a sweetheart deal with the real estate industry: a lower than market commission. And so it goes.

Get out of your lease. If you are leasing where you live now, be sure that your lease is up or you have something in writing from your landlord releasing you from your lease. It seems to be a popular belief that buying a house or moving out of town is an excuse to break a lease. It isn't. Do this before you sign the contract of purchase.

Many leases have "automatic renewal" provisions which automatically renew the lease unless you give written notice by a specified earlier date that you are leaving. Don't get trapped by this.

It is also a good idea to start looking for a home several months before your lease comes up for renewal; otherwise, you may find yourself under a lot of pressure to buy. In this regard, try to arrange with your landlord for you to go on a month-to-month basis after your lease expires, just in case you haven't located a home or aren't ready to close. This will give you a lot more flexibility.

Financial considerations. Before making an offer, figure out what the home you are considering will cost you each month to make sure you can afford it. Things to consider are your job stability, the monthly mortgage payments, taxes and insurance (all of which may change after you buy a home), as well as any dues, assessments and maintenance costs, which can be very large for many condominium units. It is often easier to *buy* a home than it is to *pay* for it.

Don't be taken in by a real estate agent's sales pitch about the taxes you will save. Just recently, a woman asked me to guide her in buying a condominium in the $90,000 range. Her accountant had said she needed to do it to save taxes. She was living in a $350 a month apartment, and the monthly cost of the condominium she wanted would be $930. At her tax bracket, I showed her that she would come out $200 per month poorer after taxes, if she bought the condominium. So, run the numbers.

The September 1983 issue of *Money* featured an article which convinced me that, in the 1980s, you will have to own your home four, five or even more years before you will come out better after taxes than you would renting. In the 1970s, when house prices were skyrocketing, the breakeven time was much shorter.

8 Espionage Work

Don't give away your weaknesses. Except for your attorney or buyer-paid real estate agent, keep strictly to yourself any information that would be useful to the seller during the contract negotiations (i.e., your lease is up in sixty days; you have already sold your home and must find another one; you are moving in from out of town and only have three days to find a home and things like that).

Such information has a way of getting back to the seller (guess how?), who can use the knowledge of your time limitations or other weaknesses to out-wait you and extract more money from you than necessary. If not before, it should be clear by now that you might not want to select a traditional real estate agent, who is a friend or relative and who knows your affairs, to assist you in finding a new home or selling your existing one. Don't forget what happened to Jill.

Investigate before signing anything. Before making any offer to buy a used home, find out everything you can about the neighborhood, schools, fire district, home and seller. *Talk to the neighbors or previous owners*, who usually love to gossip. Start by talking about general things, i.e., you are looking at the place next door and want to learn more about the area. Then, slowly work around to the home and the seller.

If only Nancy and Jill had done this. Also talk to the agent and seller. If the seller seems to be mysteriously unavailable for questioning, this should cause you to wonder if something is wrong with the home.

A careful investigation on your part should reveal the seller's weaknesses (i.e., being transferred, buying another house, getting divorced, an illness, having had the home on the market for a long time, financial problems). You might find out that the seller has an undisclosed reason for selling (i.e., a leaking basement, a highway coming through, a declining neighborhood, a high-rise going up in the next block, a changing school district, an increase in land taxes, an inefficient and expensive heating system). You may even find that the next-door neighbor is the most obnoxious person you have ever met.

If the home is For Sale By Owner, there is a better than average chance that something is wrong with it. Agents are required by their real estate licensing laws to disclose serious defects to you, and most unscrupulous sellers know this. For this reason, sellers of defective homes often do not use an agent, which Jill learned the hard way.

You will also want to know the following: what the seller paid for the house and when (to see how much leeway there is to negotiate price) and selling prices of comparable houses in the neighborhood (to see if the one you are considering is in line).

You can find out what the seller paid for the home and when by getting a copy of the seller's deed from a title insurance company or the recording department at the county courthouse. You will need the legal description of the property to do this, which the seller's agent will give you, if you are sly about it. Just say you need the legal description to be able to write an offer. If you can't get the legal description this way, you probably will be able to get it from the tax collector at the county courthouse. All you will need is the seller's name and the address of the property.

The seller's agent(s) or your own representative, if you have one, can get comparable sales for you, or you can ask around the neighborhood and do this yourself.

If, on the other hand, you are buying a newly-built house, you will again want to know comparable sales and you must check out the builder. Ask who else owns his houses and talk to them. Find out how many years the builder has been in business—the longer the better. Try to learn how many unsold houses the builder has and how long your house has been finished, which will give you a pretty good idea of whether or not the builder is in distress. The inspection department of your local government may have had some experiences with the builder, too, that might prove interesting. The last thing you want to do is to buy a house from someone like the Hope's builder.

If you are buying a condominium, town house or cooperative apartment there are special considerations: the top floors and end units are usually the quietest; the north and west facing units and top floor are usually the coldest units in winter; the west and south facing units and top floor are usually the hottest units in summer; the interior and lower units are the best insulated; the ground units are the least secure and least private; and units facing the swimming pool or parking lot, or adjoining the elevator or stairs are the noisiest.

The following legal rules, documents and property rights need to be investigated before you sign anything: mineral rights (depending on your area, who owns them may or may not be important); zoning (you don't want a high rise going up across the street); police, fire and school districts (you will want police and fire protection and to know where children in the area attend school); floodplain designation (you don't want to be in one—it will kill you on a resale, not to mention when the creek rises into your home); building lines and restrictions (which might prevent you from adding on that extra bedroom and bath); zoning restrictions (that may outlaw the garage apartment presently being rented out); restrictive covenants (which may prohibit you from fencing in your yard or adding onto your home without approval of an "architectural committee"). You can get some or all of this information with the help of the seller's agent(s) or your own representative. Or, you can go to city hall and the county courthouse and look it up yourself. You will need the street address or legal description of the property to do it.

If you are buying a condominium, town house or cooperative apartment, read the governing rules and regulations, usually called the "declarations" and "bylaws." You may find some of them do not suit you at all, such as "no pets or children allowed!" The seller or agent should be able to furnish these for you.

You should take the time to investigate any of the foregoing which apply to your situation *before* making an offer. This approach will screen out properties that ultimately will not interest you. Remember, once you have entered into the contract, it probably will be too late to change your mind.

9 *The Negotiating Process*

The agreement. The contract of purchase, the end result of the negotiations, is your most important document. You will probably be using one of the fill-in-the-blanks form sales contracts put out by a local real estate firm or title insurance company. These are a good starting point but are incomplete for you, the buyer. I make several suggestions below that you might want to add to a form contract, which you will use to make your offer. But let's first look at how a contract is born.

Your signed offer will be presented to the seller, who, in all probability will make written changes (more favorable to the seller, of course), and send it back. This is called making a "counteroffer." If you like it, then you have a deal. If not, then you can make more changes in place and send it back to the seller (another counteroffer). This could happen several times before an agreement is reached. If an agreement is reached and the contract is too messy to read, draw up a fresh one with just the final facts and figures on it. In either event, make sure the rules of the next paragraph are followed to the letter. It would be best for a lawyer to do this.

All agreements pertaining to the sale of real estate (meaning a home) must be in writing and signed by the buyer and seller, else they are void. And any changes made in place on a contract should be *initialed* by all parties to it, or there is no agreement. So, if you want certain financing or the right to inspect the home before the closing, or anything else, put it in the contract. **No verbal agreements, period.** Finally, the signed and initialled agreement, or a copy of it, must be delivered to you (or your representatives) and the seller to seal the deal.

Be a shrewd bargainer. Many books have been written about negotiating, and you should read one. In general, disclose as little as possible about yourself and learn as much as possible about the seller. The more you know about the seller and the less the seller knows about you, the stronger your bargaining position will be. You should also be patient, polite and act understanding of the seller's needs, while being firm about your own. Finally, find out what the seller's deadlines are (date being transferred out of town, date contract on seller's next home will expire, etc.), and let them force the seller to come to you. The closer the seller is to his or her deadlines, the more concessions you will get.

Four other rules of good negotiating should be mentioned here: (1) if you aren't willing to risk losing the house, you will not be able to negotiate well; (2) get the seller and his or her agent(s) to invest as much time in you as possible, which will make them concede more if it looks like you are going to go away; (3) the longer an agent has been working on the deal, the sicker he or she will be of it and the more he or she will pressure the seller to make concessions to you; and (4) set a top limit in your mind that you will pay and stick to it.

The concessions you will get from the seller may also depend on other factors such as: how well homes are moving in general; how long the seller's home has been on the market; whether the seller is trying to buy another home; whether the seller is in distress; whether you can make an offer that will not require the seller to hold paper; whether you can make an offer that does not hinge on something iffy, like selling your home; how much the seller has in the home; whether there is a competing buyer, and so forth. If you are buying a newly-built home, find out how many unsold homes the builder has. The more houses there are, the weaker the builder will be. But remember what happened to the Hopes with a weak builder.

Often you can gain the advantage in the negotiations by sitting down face-to-face with the seller. This is especially true when you are familiar with the subject matter and the seller is not. Real estate agents can almost always get the seller a better deal than the seller can get alone, and this is one reason the seller's agent will not want you to see the seller during the negotiations. You can get around this very easily by saying that you will not proceed with the negotiations unless the seller is present. Bargaining face-to-face with the seller is usually most productive after the negotiations have been going on for a while and you have gotten the seller or his or her agent really interested in your making a deal.

As to the actual negotiations, most people will expect you to bargain[1], so do not be afraid to offer less than the asking price. Be careful, though. An offer that is too low may make the seller mad and kill any chance to reach a compromise, especially when the seller has made previous reductions in the price, or is asking less than what was paid for the home.

Normally, I find that somewhere between 85 and 90 percent of the asking price usually is a good *first* offer on a used home. On a newly-built home, I usually start a little over 90 percent of the builder's asking price, because builders generally do not have as much room to negotiate.

For instance, if the seller of a used home is asking $100,000, the taking price is probably in the low to mid 90s, so make an offer in the mid 80s. Then increase the amount of your offers

1. Again, referring to the 1983 Birmingham statistics, on the average, *listed* homes that sold that year went for 94 percent of the list (asking) price. This included used and newly-built homes.

to a predetermined target price, $93,000, above which you will not go. If it's a newly-built home, start at $91,000, planning to go as high as $96,000.

You might also decide to give up some of the provisions in your offer to which the seller has strong objections. Each thing you give up, though, should be matched by a concession in price, terms, and so on by the seller. Let the seller know he or she is buying the protection you are giving up.

A technique I like to use for buyers when there isn't a threat of a competing buyer, or when it's a slow market, is to never accept the seller's offer, even if it is at a price my client will pay. Here's why. Suppose you offer $74,000 on an $82,500 home and the seller counters $78,000, a price you will pay. If you accept the $78,000, you have lost the opportunity to get the home for $76,000 or $77,000. So make another offer at $76,000 and wait. You are the only one (I hope) that knows you will pay $78,000.

Unless there is a competing buyer, there is little risk in doing this, because the seller isn't going anywhere. On the other hand, your money is very portable, and the seller may be getting worried about you tiring of the game. If the seller accepts the $76,000, you have a deal. If the seller counters for $77,000, counter back $76,500 and wait again. You can also use this technique to negotiate the amount and terms of any paper the seller might hold, what appliances will go with the home, and so on.

You should already know by this time in the transaction what some of the seller's weaknesses are, but you can create some additional ones for the seller to swing the momentum your way. One way is to let it be known that you are considering buying another home, which creates an artificial deadline for the seller.

Real estate agents do this to buyers all the time saying, "Someone else is going to make an offer, so you had better make one if you want the home!" But if an agent says this to you, just back off for a while. If the home sells to someone else in a few days, then there was another buyer. If it doesn't, then there wasn't one. Regardless, the last thing you want is to get into a bidding war and run up the price. But, you say, "What if it's the home of my dreams?" My answer probably would be, "Dreams can get expensive." Nevertheless, this is a valid consideration that has cost many emotional buyers money.

Another way to create a deadline for the seller is to write into your offer that it will expire after twenty-four hours. Such an offer not only puts pressure on the seller to act quickly and, hopefully, not too wisely, it also restricts the seller's ability to "shop" your offer to another buyer that also might be interested in the seller's home.

Finally, if the negotiations get bogged down, you might try making a final take-it-or-leave-it offer. If the seller or agent really think you are going to walk away after all of the time and effort they have put into you, each will start thinking about making additional concessions to get an agreement.

If there is an agent, if would not be out of line at this time for you to suggest, preferably in the seller's presence, that a deal might be struck if the agent would cut the commission to allow the seller to lower the price of the home. Another way to get this idea across to the seller is to write a lower commission into your next offer. The way to do this is described in the next section. The seller may not have the guts to suggest reducing the commission or even know that commissions are negotiable at this point in time. Buying a home is serious business.

To conclude the discussion on negotiating, I offer this checklist of important points.

Shrewd Bargaining Checklist
1. Always be prepared to walk away from the deal.
2. Set a top limit above which you will not go.

3. Try to be in a position to make an offer that is not iffy, i.e., hinges on something that is not likely to happen soon, like selling your home.
4. Do intelligence work on the seller.
5. Say as little as possible about yourself.
6. Do not be afraid to make a low first offer and do not allow a seller's agent to talk you out of doing it.
7. Be patient, nice and hide your emotions (if you can't, you should hire your own representative to negotiate for you).
8. Get the seller and his or her agent(s) to invest a lot of time in you.
9. Let the seller's deadlines give the seller a nervous headache, to be made into an "Excederin headache" by giving the seller's agent(s) time to work over the seller.
10. Create additional deadlines for the seller.
11. Don't fall for the old "there's another buyer" trick.
12. Negotiate the commission for the seller.
13. Make the seller accept your offer.

Cutting out an agent. If you are working with a traditional agent, as Jill was, and find a home on your own that you want to see, do you have to bring your agent into the deal? Absolutely not, although you may feel morally obligated to do so, especially if the agent is a friend or relative. You can save a lot of money going directly to the listing agent or owner, as the case may be. Here's how.

If the home is listed with an agent, go to the listing agent and ask if the commission can be reduced (because it will not be co-oped) to allow the seller to reduce the asking price. If the agent agrees to this, mentally knock one-half the commission off the asking price before deciding on your offer price, and write into the offer what the new commission will be to alert the seller to what is happening. If the agent will not agree to reduce the commission, you can force the issue by making the offer as described (or you can speak directly to the seller about it). The agent, you can be sure, will object, but the law and the rules of the National Association of Realtors® require that your offer be presented as written. Next, the agent and seller will start arguing over who will give up what to make a deal with you.

For example, if the asking price is $100,000 and the commission is $6,000, assume a $97,000 asking price, then make an offer of 85 percent of $97,000, or $82,450, and write the new commission percentage or amount into the blank space provided in the contract.

If the home is For Sale By Owner, tell the owner that you are mentally reducing the asking price because there isn't a commission. The owner may say the home is priced net of a commission, but don't believe it. Treat the owner like the listing agent, entitled to one-half of a commission, and make an offer similar to that given in the example.

You will not be able to cut out the listing agent altogether, because the seller will owe a commission regardless of who produces a buyer. If you have hired your own agent, you will have to pay the agreed commission (whether a percentage, flat rate or hourly charge) even if you deal directly with the listing agent or owner. So, keep these points in mind when you are thinking about cutting out an agent.

10 Protective Provisions

Earnest money. More than likely, you will put up a deposit, called "earnest money," when you make your offer. This is a custom, not a legal requirement, showing your good faith.

Do not give this money to the seller until the closing. It is still your money until that time. If a real estate agent is involved, your earnest money will be held in the bank account of the agent's real estate firm or with a local title insurance company. If no agent is involved, you should set up your own escrow (trust) account with either a title insurance company or with a bank. The escrow agent will hold the earnest money until the closing or until the deal falls through, paying it at that time to whichever party is then entitled to it.

If you are making an offer that is contingent on something happening, such as getting financing, selling your existing home, or a satisfactory inspection, write this into your offer. Also state in your offer that, if the contingency event does not occur, you can call off the deal and get your earnest money back.

Some people think putting up a lot of earnest money enables them to get more concessions from the seller. To some extent this is probably true. But if you are making an offer contingent on getting certain financing, an inspection, selling your existing home and so on, the amount of earnest money is irrelevant as long as the contingency is in place, because you do not have to close until it is satisfied. Furthermore, if something unexpected comes up which will prevent you from being able to close, such as your spouse informing you at breakfast about your impending divorce, you may end up leaving a lot more money on the table than you can afford to loose.

You will not earn interest on your earnest money unless the contract of purchase says you do. So, if you want to earn interest, write it into the contract.

Personal property that you want. Removable items such as the draperies, standing refrigerator, window air-conditioning units, and so on, are not considered real estate and do not go with the house, unless the contract of purchase provides for such items to remain. If you want these, write it into the contract. Attached items such as the wall-to-wall carpeting, light fixtures and attic fan are considered part of the house, and you automatically get these unless otherwise stated in the contract.

What about the children's swing set in the back yard? Does it go with the house? I don't know. To be completely safe, write into the contract everything that you want to stay with the house that could easily be carried off.

Closing costs. Costs of closing the transaction, such as the lender's loan fee, the closing attorney's fee, the cost of the survey and title insurance, etc., can add up to a lot of money. The contract of purchase should state who is to pay them. Otherwise, you will end up arguing about it at the closing. The real estate agent or mortgage lender can give you a good estimate of these costs ahead of time.

If you are obtaining a new loan from a commercial lender, you will come out ahead adding the closing costs to the agreed price of the home and having the seller pay them at closing.

For example, assume an $80,000 sales price, 75 percent loan, two discount points, two loan fee points, and $600 dollars (estimated) in other closing costs.

If you pay the closing costs, it looks like this:

Sales price	$ 80,000
Less loan (.75 × $80,000)	− 60,000
Down payment	20,000
Plus: Points (.04 × $60,000)	2,400
Other costs	+ 600
Cash to close	$23,000

But if you add them on to the price and the seller pays them, it looks like this:

Sales price	$80,000
Plus: Points (.04 × $60,000)	2,400
Other costs	+ 600
Revised sales price	$83,000
Less revised loan (.75 × $83,000)	− 62,250
Cash to close	$20,750
Savings ($23,000 − $20,750)	$ 2,250

This doesn't cost the seller anything. The cost to you is a slightly larger mortgage ($2,250) and the lost tax deduction for the discount. (Remember, only discount points are tax deductible). If you are in the present maximum 50 percent tax bracket, you lose $600 in tax savings (.50 × $1,200) *next* April 15. You are still $1,650 ahead ($2,250 − $600).

You may have noticed that this last example isn't entirely accurate, because the dollar amount of the points would change on a larger loan; but so would everything else, in small and ever decreasing amounts ad infinitum. So, you add to the sales price an approximation of what you think the closing costs will be. Consider having a side agreement with the seller for any adjustments that have to be made once the actual costs are known. These agreements are often illegal but are common in practice. You will have to decide whether or not to use one. If you do, don't tell anyone about it.

Contract inspection provisions. If you are buying a used home, make the contract of purchase contingent on an inspection of the home which is satisfactory to you. It is your money, so you should be the one who is satisfied. Do not rely on phrases that are usually put in contracts by real estate agents such as: "Seller warrants that all systems and appliances will be in good working order at closing." Such provisions do not cover many of the things that can go wrong, and the little protection that they do offer usually ends at the closing.

An example of an inspection provision I like to use follows. Leave the second sentence about the time limit out, unless the seller insists on a deadline for the inspection.

> This contract is contingent on an inspection of the premises which is satisfactory to Buyer. The inspection shall be deemed unsatisfactory, unless Buyer notifies Seller or Seller's agent(s) within _____ days from the contract date that the inspection is satisfactory to Buyer.

The second sentence automatically lets you out by inaction. This protects you if something comes up and you are unable to make the inspection within the required time. Of course, you can always renegotiate a later time to inspect.

As to the actual inspection of a *used home*, you will want to wait until *after* you have made a deal with the seller before you have it done. There are two reasons for this. First, you will not like spending money for an inspection on a house you may never own. Second, you may be able to use the inspection results to *renegotiate* the deal, which is discussed later. You also should have your inspection done after a hard rain and during daylight hours, if you want to find out about water problems and be able to see what you are inspecting. How to do the inspection is discussed later.

If you are considering buying a *newly-built house*, make the contract of purchase "contingent on the house being completed in accordance with local building and health codes, utility company requirements and the plans and specifications." If the house is a newly-built or converted condominium (town house or cooperative apartment), you should also make the contract contingent on all of the units being completed, not just yours. Otherwise, if the builder gets in trouble, you might end up living in a half-finished complex.

You should also provide in the contract that you are to receive a copy of the house plans and building specifications when the deal is made. Otherwise, you will have a difficult time monitoring the construction or determining that the house was built as agreed.

Do not put up the money for the land or the cost of construction (as the Hopes did), unless the builder can furnish a "performance bond" satisfactory to you. The last thing you want is for the builder to quit on you halfway through the job after spending a lot of your money. The bond will insure that someone else will come in and finish the work at no additional cost to you other than that called for in the contract. Use a qualified insurance agent for this. You will find that most builders cannot obtain a performance bond because of their financial condition, a fact that will be good to know up front.

Progress inspections should be made on a house that is being built at least weekly. Otherwise, if the builder misreads the plans, or simply chooses not to follow them, it will be too late to correct any mistakes. The final inspection should be made immediately prior to closing, during daylight hours and just after a hard rain, if possible. The specifics of the inspection are discussed later.

The seller's written promises. Include the following provision in any contract of purchase to buy a *used home*:

> Seller promises Buyer that, except for those items listed below, the home (refer to it as the unit if it is a condominium, town house or cooperative apartment) will be delivered to Buyer free from major defects, tidy and with all systems and appliances in good repair, normal wear and tear excepted.
>
> The existing defects are: (list them here)

This provision will virtually eliminate caveat emptor from your transaction, because it gives you the legal right, which you would not ordinarily have, to seek reimbursement from the seller after the closing for major defects that your inspection does not reveal or that the seller does not know of or tell you about. Some defects are hidden, such as an underpowered air-conditioning system in a home you are buying in December, rotten wood that has been painted over or a well that sometimes dries up in the summer. More important, this provision is good at flushing out dishonest sellers (like Nancy's and Jill's), who will not, for obvious reasons, want it in the contract of purchase. You should be wary—very wary—of any seller who will not agree to it.

If you are buying a *newly-built home*, use this provision instead:

> Seller promises Buyer that the home (refer to it as the unit if it is a condominium, town house or cooperative apartment) and any related structures will be built in a good and workmanlike manner, according to code, standard practices, and the plans and specifications or any written and signed changes thereto; that the construction will be complete, all required governmental approvals obtained, all utilities turned on, and all debris removed by the time of closing.

You want this provision in addition to the inspection contingency provision suggested in the contract inspection provision in the preceding section. The inspection contingency provision only allows you to stall the closing until everything *appears* to be finished, or get out of the deal if it isn't. Whereas, the promise suggested above gives you the legal right to go after the builder following the closing, if it turns out that things are not what they appeared to be.

As previously mentioned, the consumer protection laws of most states have relaxed, to some extent, the caveat emptor rule in the new home area, but this suggested provision is stronger than most of those laws and is in addition to them. Also, it is in writing. Many of the new home consumer protection laws have been created by court decisions on a case-by-case basis, rather than by a statute written by the state legislature. Therefore, it is not always entirely clear what these consumer protection laws do or do not cover.

If you are buying a *newly-converted condominium*, which is part used and part new construction, combine the provisions suggested for both used and newly-built homes to make sure that you are covered.

After-the-closing protection. It is, of course, very important that you are protected *after the closing* for things that might go wrong but which you will not discover until you move in, or even later. The seller's written promises only give you legal protection that you might have to go to court to enforce. This isn't very practical. Sellers can really surprise you. For instance, in one case I handled, the sellers took the central vacuum system when they moved out!

The easiest and best way to avoid having to go through the hassle of litigation to enforce your legal rights is to get the seller or builder to agree in the contract of purchase to hold paper from you after the closing for part of the purchase price. You do this even though you are able to buy without the seller or builder holding paper.

The seller of a used home will be encouraged to disclose all of its defects. If any are not disclosed, you will have practical rights (unlike Nancy or Jill) and can just quit paying until you get back what the seller owes you. Therefore, you will not want to tell the seller why you really want to use paper. This is, of course, a classic Mexican standoff. You owe the seller money, but you can sue for fraud, which discourages the seller from trying to collect what you owe. If things ever get to this point, hire a lawyer.

Using this version of the Golden Rule will also protect you from a builder, who might otherwise be "too busy" to complete the work. Too bad the Hopes don't owe their builder money.

Another way to protect yourself after the closing, which is not as good as getting the seller to hold paper, is to require in the contract of purchase that an escrow (trust fund) be set aside out of the part of the money that you pay at closing (this is what Nancy was trying to do). The escrow would last for a reasonable period of time (the longer, the better for you) after the closing to enable you to move in and determine that the home was delivered to you as promised (or determine the cause of and repair a known problem.)

You can virtually count on the seller and the real estate agent "howling" about this kind of arrangement, so be prepared. Tell them that what you want is no different from them wanting earnest money up front from you to insure that you honor the contract. You want earnest money for the same reason, but at the end. Who can argue with that? The seller might agree to this more readily if you suggest that the money to be held back will be the real estate commission and not the seller's net proceeds. The drawbacks to an escrow are that it usually expires too soon, and if you and the seller get into an argument, it is tough to get the money released. An example of an escrow clause I use is:

> _____ dollars of the sales proceeds shall be held back by the closing agent until _____ days after possession of the home has been delivered to Buyer. The held back funds shall then be paid by the closing agent to Seller, unless Buyer has notified the closing agent in writing that the home was not delivered by Seller as required by the sales contract. If that occurs, the closing agent shall hold said funds until the dispute is resolved in writing between Buyer and Seller.

Another way to protect yourself is to get the seller to let you move in before the closing. This is a really dumb thing for the seller to do, but it sometimes happens. Once you are in, you will find out if things are as promised. If they aren't, you can stall until any problems are corrected or the seller makes whatever concessions you want to make you feel better.

Yet another way to get protection after the closing is to buy, or better still, get the seller to buy one of the commercial home warranties that are now available. The home warranty industry started in the early 1970s. Some of the earlier companies went bankrupt and did not honor their warranties. Those in business now are too new for us to judge whether or not they will last. However, the warranties that they offer are reasonable in cost and cover some, but not all, of the major things that can go wrong with the systems in a home. They do not cover such things as the seller taking the swing set or central vacuum system in violation of the contract of purchase, or not moving out after the closing on the agreed date.

Most real estate agents will know about home warranty companies, and many get sellers and builders to offer home warranty protection as an inducement to potential home buyers. Be sure to check out the features of the warranty agreement and talk with some people who have made claims against the warranty company before signing the contract of purchase.

In summary, just remember that once the seller has all of your money, the "horse is out of the barn," and, like Nancy and Jill, you may well be undone. You do not see many sellers or builders voluntarily cough up money after the closing, and a lawsuit is not a satisfactory solution in most cases. Litigation is expensive, time-consuming and nerve-wracking, and the only ones who usually gain from it are lawyers. Having practical after-the-closing protection is a much better remedy for you.

The possession date. If the seller will not move out until after the closing, which is normally what happens, provide in the contract of purchase that the seller will owe you some stated amount of rent for the days he or she stays in the home after the closing. Otherwise, you will be paying for the seller's lodging during that time.

I find it best to give the seller a little time after the closing to move out. This gives you more flexibility to deal with any problems that go unresolved until the eve of closing. Remember, if your movers are already on the way, it will be hard to wait out the seller.

11 Traps for the Unwary

The Statute of Frauds. You have noticed that I am fond of putting everything in writing. I do this for two reasons: first, it's very difficult to prove anything that is not in writing; and second, when it comes to buying and selling real estate (which includes a home), verbal agreements, under an ancient rule of law called the "Statute of Frauds," are illegal. In other words, gentlemen's agreements are unenforceable. I have seen many unsuspecting home buyers sadly discover this at the closing, or even afterwards.

Describe your financing. If you are going to be getting any financing to buy the home, state in the contract of purchase precisely what the financing is to be (and the number of points, if you are to pay them) and that you can call off the deal if you do not get it. Financing covers taking out a new loan, either with the seller or a commercial lender, as well as taking over an existing loan, as in an equity sale. What you are told you will get and what actually happens often are different, invariably at your expense.

If the financing turns out to be less favorable than you require, you will be in a position to ask for concessions from the seller or agents to compensate you for it, i.e., the seller holding a little more paper, reducing the price or down payment and so forth. Or, you can call the whole thing off. The threat of your doing just that can have remarkable effects, for you, on the seller and agent(s).

Equity sales. Remember, if the mortgage has an alienation clause and the home is sold without the lender's approval, then the lender can either call the loan, make you pay points and a higher interest rate or foreclose.

I have seen several cute and dangerous ways used to get around due-on-sale and alienation provisions, usually at the suggestion of the seller's real estate agent. I don't think any of the suggested methods I have seen would have withstood a foreclosure action by the lender. Until the courts in your state rule this type of provision to be invalid or your state legislature outlaws them, don't try to get around them. This is a very dangerous area.

Balloon financing. This has already been discussed, but it is so dangerous that is deserves mentioning again. Unless you like playing roulette for very high stakes, or are very wealthy, try to avoid agreeing to any mortgage financing that contains a balloon provision. Remember the Wilts who are still sweating it out.

Attorney fees for breach of contract. Unless the contract of purchase says that you can, most states do not allow the recovery of attorney fees or suit expenses for breach of contract or promise. These expenses can be very large, and you may want this protection. In most cases, it will be the seller who breaches the contract or isn't truthful. If you put such a provision into your contract of purchase, be sure that you aren't likely to breach the contract, or you will regret your decision. An example of such a provision is the following:

> Should Buyer or Seller breach this agreement, then the party not in breach shall be entitled to recover, among

other damages, a reasonable attorney's fee and litigation expenses.

My feeling is that using a provision like this will spook a seller. You will probably come out better in the negotiations without it, but later on you may wish you had included it.

Limit your exposure. If you breach the contract and do not close, you could lose a lot more than your earnest money. In most states, the seller can ask a court to require that you close or put you in jail for being in contempt of court (called "specific performance"), or the seller can sell the home to someone else and sue you for any loss incurred as a result of your failure to close. For instance, I recently handled a case for a seller against a change-of-heart buyer, and the poor buyer ended up buying two homes, my client's and the one he agreed to buy after thinking he could walk away from his agreement with them.

I have never known a home buyer who was aware of this and have heard many real estate agents sheepishly say to a very upset buyer that they did not know it either. You can limit your exposure by writing in the contract of purchase a statement that your liability is limited to your earnest money or some other fixed amount. The *form* sales contracts previously mentioned usually do not contain this protective wording. They are drawn up by lawyers who represent real estate companies (which represent the seller) and not you.

Hazard insurance. Require in the contract of purchase (most form real estate sales contracts do) that the seller will carry sufficient hazard insurance to protect your interests until the closing. (It insures against fire, storm and other disasters.) Otherwise, if the home burns down before the closing, there will be a big problem if you can't find a comparable home for the same price. When you close, you should have your own homeowners insurance which contains hazard as well as several other types of coverage. Let a qualified insurance agent advise you in this area.

Distress sales. Some people try to buy homes that have been sold in foreclosure or for the nonpayment of debts or taxes. This can be a good way to buy a home for much less than its value. Most states have laws, though, that give the prior owner the right to buy the property back from you, whether or not you want to sell. This is called the "right of redemption." The right of redemption can run for a year or more, so be aware of this potential problem if you are planning to buy a distress sale home. Also bear in mind, whenever you buy this type of home, you will be buying *as is*. For this reason, you will have to rely completely on your inspection to ferret out the problems. There won't be any after-the-closing protection.

Good distress sales are easier to find during or just following severe downturns in the economy. This is when most builders go broke and have to give their houses under construction back to the bank. It is also when most unemployment occurs, which leads to homeowners being unable to pay their mortgages. To find out about builders' houses being foreclosed, call the real estate departments of your local banks. To find out about other homes being foreclosed, look in your newspapers, where the foreclosure ads are run. Then call the lender to get the details. Remember, if the loan foreclosed was FHA or VA, you will have to go through a real estate firm.

12   *Title Matters*

Title documents. Require that the seller agrees in the contract of purchase to give you a "warranty deed" and "good and marketable title." This, along with title insurance and a survey will protect your title.

Before going to law school I bought a home and agreed to take a quitclaim deed from the seller. This type of deed contains no title warranties and conveys only what interest in the property the seller owns, which may be no interest at all. It was the real estate agent's idea to use a quitclaim deed, and you should never agree to one.

Title protection. Require in the contract of purchase that you be furnished a *title insurance policy.* Most form contracts will provide for this. Title insurance will protect your title up to the amount of the coverage for everything except the right of redemption, matters that would be disclosed by a survey, and unfiled mechanic's liens (unpaid claims for work or materials that do not show up until after the closing). Some title insurance companies will insure against unfiled mechanic's liens for a small additional premium. Another way you can protect yourself against unfiled mechanic's liens is to owe the seller money after the closing.

As your property goes up in value, you might consider increasing the title insurance coverage. Most title insurance companies do not automatically raise it for you. For instance, if you buy a $50,000 home, your title insurance will only be for that amount even though the home's value later increases to $70,000. For an additional premium, you can increase the coverage to $70,000.

In some areas, a *lawyer's opinion of title* is used instead of title insurance. This, to me, is a weak second choice. Suppose, for instance, that the lawyer fouls something up and doesn't have malpractice insurance? Or, what if the lawyer's insurance carrier gets cute and tries to get you to settle for less than your loss? Title insurance companies, at least the larger ones, do not offer these risks.

Survey. Require in the contract of purchase that you be furnished a clean survey at the closing. A survey shows the land and all improvements (including the home) that have been made to it and whether or not the property is located in a floodplain. Since your title insurance does not insure against matters of survey, you will want to know before paying your money that your property is ten acres as promised, and not six acres, that you home is not in the water works' right-of-way or over the property line, that the neighbor's driveway is not ten feet over on your property or that the home isn't located in a floodplain. I have seen many homes with these and other horrible problems that could have been disclosed in advance by a survey.

13 *After Making a Deal*

You have now reached an agreement and there are some things that you must do to get ready to close.

First, do your inspection as described below.

Next, if you are getting a commercial loan, then the burden is on you to make every effort to get it, i.e., apply for it with a commercial lender. If you are working with a traditional agent or have your own representative, they will help you do this.

Then, start making arrangements to be moved, but leave yourself some flexibility so you can remain in a strong position time-wise until the closing.

The inspection. Now that you have gotten this far it is time for the inspection. Whether you are buying a used or newly-built home, *use professionals* for the inspections, unless you know how to do them. This may cost you some money, but it's good insurance. A professional inspector may not catch everything, but by using one your odds will be improved considerably. Try to arrange for the inspections to be made during the daytime and after a hard rain; this is when most defects and water problems will be found.

The inspection of a *used home* should cover the following:

(1) The structure, roof, attic, and basement or crawl area.

(2) All systems, i.e., plumbing, wiring, heating and cooling, septic and well. *Talk to the neighbors* (if you are buying a

condominium, the members of the condominium association) and whoever has been servicing the systems. This will often reveal problems that an inspection will not, such as a basement that leaks during the rainy season, a septic field that doesn't drain properly in wet weather, or a well that dries up in the summer or water which isn't potable.

(3) Wood damage by termites, wood borers, beetles, ants or dry rot. A pest-control bond on the home should be disregarded. Many homes covered by such "pieces of paper" have been eaten up by pests or seriously damaged by dry rot. And many so-called bonds provide no more coverage than a promise to treat again, not to repair. Get a "wood infestation" inspection, such as those that are required for all VA and FHA loans. Any pest control company can do this, but if you want an impartial inspection don't use the one that is already servicing the home.

(4) Energy efficiency. Look at the last twelve months' utility bills. If possible, get the local utility company to do an energy audit and to offer energy-conserving recommendations. You may find that the home is not energy efficient and that the cost of making it efficient will be prohibitive. Find out if the home has asbestos or formaldehyde-based insulation in the attic or in the walls. A lot of people are scared to death of the stuff and, although there may be nothing wrong with it, it will probably hurt you if you ever sell the home. I know a lawyer who lost $15,000 on the sale of his home because of formaldehyde insulation he had blown into the walls.

(5) Solar energy. If you plan to add a solar retrofit, such as a greenhouse, solar panels or collectors, make sure that there are no obstructions between the sun and the home. Remember, the sun travels at a much lower angle in the sky in the winter. The neighboring house, which doesn't block the sunlight in September, may catch two or three hours of it in the winter when you need it. Consider the possibility that future con-

struction on land adjoining yours could block your sunlight. At the present, there is little, if any, legal protection against this. Finally, make sure that your planned solar addition will not violate any building or set-back line codes.

Before closing on a *newly-built* home, you should do the following:

(1) Obtain a certificate of completion of construction from the local building and health departments. Some local governments do not require or provide this. If the home that you are considering buying is in one of these localities, then you will be at the mercy of the builder. This is when the builder's reputation will be very important, not to mention his or her financial condition.

(2) Make sure that all utilities have been turned on. If they haven't been, this could mean that the construction does not satisfy the requirements of one or more of the utility companies. Taking a cold shower in the dark in December is no fun!

(3) Review the plans and specifications to determine that the construction is in full compliance. Remember the Hopes' air-conditioning ducts weren't insulated, although the specifications required it.

A *last-minute walk-through* by you just prior to the closing is a *must*. A *surprise* last-minute walk-through is even better. You might catch the seller taking down the dining room chandelier or taking out the attic fan, or you might learn that the builder didn't have the utilities turned on or all the uncompleted items finished, although he had promised the day before that it would be done "first thing in the morning!"

With the suggested inspection wording in the contract of purchase, you will have several choices if you are not satisfied with the results of the inspection. You can go ahead with the purchase and bear the loss that the defects will cause to the value of the home. You can call off the deal. Or, you can give the seller or builder the choice of correcting the defects—if they can be corrected—or reducing the price of the home to repay you for its lower value caused by the defects.

You may even be able to get the real estate agent to cut his or her commission, so that the seller can lower the price. The deeper you are into the transaction at this point in time, the more time and effort the seller or builder and the real estate agent will have invested in you and the more dollar concessions you should be able to get from them for you to close. Remember, you are making a substantial investment, not trying to win a popularity contest.

Time is of the essence. Neither party has to close by the agreed date, unless the contract of purchase states that "time is of the essence." The courts have held that, without this statement in the contract, the parties are only required to close within a reasonable time after the agreed closing date. Few people know this, and you can bet that no traditional real estate agent will tell you about it.

If something comes up that you did not expect and you need more time before you close, you can use this rule to delay the closing several weeks in most states. I have seen this done when buyers were waiting on their existing homes to close or for interest rates to comes down, or even to try to gain additional concessions from the seller. Remember, though, that the seller can use the rule against you, too.

Do not close until you are good and ready. Insist on seeing the closing documents at least one day prior to closing so that you can review them at your leisure. They will be unfamiliar to you, and the closing will go too quickly for you to keep up if you haven't done this.

If there is anything in dispute or left undone, stall going to the closing until it is resolved. The last place to argue is at the closing when the movers are on the way or, like Nancy, you have a flight to catch.

If something does come up at the closing, expect to get a lot of pressure from the real estate agent, closing agent or the seller for you to close first and to resolve your questions later. With the finish line in sight, you will be tempted to cut corners or give in to make the others think you are a "nice guy." Do not fall into this trap. Close only after you are satisfied that everything is in order. Nancy didn't do this.

The closing. You and your opponents will attend the closing, you with your money and they with their hands out. If everything is in order, make arrangements with the seller or builder about the possession date, transfer of utilities, keys and warranties (roof, septic, appliance and pest control). Then sign the papers, pay the closing agent, go home and start getting ready to move.

Conclusion

Although I could tell you many more sad tales, the suggestions I have made should give you a lot of protection when buying a home. What has been presented came from many unpleasant client experiences. They simply failed to view buying a home as making a substantial investment, a serious game requiring preparation, patience and a cool head. Unlike them, I hope that you will be able to buy a home, not a problem, at the best possible price. You now have the potential to play wolf—so, good hunting!

ON SELLING YOUR: Home, $weet Home

After I wrote this, many of my real estate friends suggested that I also write something about selling homes. We knew that sellers were also being taken advantage of.

At first, I was hesitant to write anything that might make things even more difficult for home buyers. Then I realized that nearly everyone who buys a home eventually sells it and that I had covered only one-half of a very important subject. So, I wrote *ON SELLING YOUR: Home, $weet Home* using the same critical, contrarian approach taken here.

Now the story is complete; all secrets told.

Contract Instructions

I spent a lot of time trying to figure out how to present a form contract which could be used for an offer. Unfortunately, local customs, practices and laws of home buying vary so much that I found it impossible to design a contract that would have universal application. I also have a feeling that, if you present a contract offer that doesn't look like what agents and sellers in your area are used to seeing, you might scare them to death. For that reason, it seems best to modify and use one of the fill-in-the-blank form contracts put out by the local real estate and title insurance companies.

There are two ways to modify these contracts: striking through wording you do not like and adding wording favorable to you. Any wording you strike through should be initialed by you. To add wording, just use a separate piece of paper and staple it to the form contract.

Here is some sample wording that you may want to strike out of a form contract:

> The Agent makes no representation or warranty of any kind as to the condition of the subject property.

> Seller's obligation to Buyer for the condition of the home ends at closing (or delivery of possession).

> Buyer shall pay all loan closing costs.

The provision that follows is an example of how to add wording:

> This is an addition to and a part of that contract for the purchase by _____ from _____ of the home located at _____ .

> 1. Buyer's duty to close is contingent on an inspection satisfactory to Buyer.

> 2. Buyer's duty to close is contingent on Buyer obtaining a thirty-year 90 percent conventional loan at an interest rate not to exceed 12 percent and with total points not to exceed 4 percent of the loan amount.

> 3. Seller promises Buyer that, except for those items listed below, the home will be delivered to Buyer free from major defects, tidy, and with all systems and appliances in good repair, normal wear and tear excepted.

> The existing defects are:

> Failure of any contingency stated above will give Buyer the right to void this contract and receive a full refund of the earnest money.

_____   _____
Buyer   Seller

Settlement Costs

The following is an outline of the various types of costs that are involved in a typical home buying transaction. Those costs which apply to a new loan will not apply to an assumption (equity purchase). The remaining costs apply to either type of transaction. The outline is set up as a simplified closing statement. Fill in the appropriate blanks and add the figures to get the estimated settlement costs. Add your down payment to that to get your total estimated cash requirement.

Closing Costs

New loan discount (except VA loans) _____

New loan service/origination fee _____

New loan appraisal fee _____

Credit report _____

Mortgage assumption fee _____

New loan amortization schedule _____

New loan photographs _____

Closing agent's fee _____

Title insurance premium (or lawyer's

    title opinion) _____

Recording fees _____

    Deed _____

    Mortgage _____

    Other _____

Survey _____

New loan inspection/appraisal fee _____

Total closing costs _____

Prorations:

Property taxes   _____

Interest   _____

Insurance   _____

Association dues   _____

Garbage/sewer fee   _____

Utilities   _____

Escrow account (impound)   _____

Other   _____

                                    Total prorations _____

Prepaid Items on New Loan

Prepaid interest   _____

Hazard (homeowner) insurance premium   _____

Mortgage insurance premium   _____

Escrow deposits   _____

    2 months hazard insurance   _____

    2 months mortgage insurance   _____

    2 months taxes   _____

                                      Total prepaids _____

                             Total settlement costs _____

Down payment   _____

                            Total cash requirement   _____

Index